ANTIQUE TRADER'S

CASHING IN
YOUR COLLECTIBLES

ANTIQUE TRADER BO
A DIVISION OF LANDMARK SPECIALTY PUBLICATIONS
NORFOLK, VIRGINIA

ANTIQUE TRADER'S
CASHING IN
YOUR COLLECTIBLES

BY MIRIAM PLANS

ISBN: 1-58221-003-9
Library of Congress Catalog Card Number: 98-89969

Editor: Wendy Chia-Klesch
Copy Editor: Sandra Holcombe
Art Director & Cover: Chris Decker
Graphic Designer: Cheryl L. Wagner
Illustrator: Jason Kofke

Printed in the United States of America

To order additional copies of this book, or to obtain a catalog, please contact:

Antique Trader Books P.O. Box 1050 Dubuque, Iowa 52004
1-800-334-7165
www.collect.com

CONTENTS

Sooner or later, probably every one of us will have to take stock of our possessions with the idea of cashing in on or disposing of all those accumulated "things." These might be items you once thought you could not live without. But the time has come to clear the decks because you are in a situation like one of the following:

- You are moving into smaller living quarters.
- You are dissolving your marriage and dividing up the property.
- You have a new job and are relocating to another part of the country/world.
- You need money instead of all those articles.
- You are entering a retirement or nursing home.
- You are widowed.
- You have lost interest in these types of items and are attracted to a different category of collectibles.
- You have inherited all of grandma's household effects and don't know what to do with them.
- You were named executor of an estate.
- The final blow — your children don't want your things.

Distributing or emptying your house of a stockpile of unrelated furniture, artifacts, and sundries is a big undertaking. It can affect you financially and emotionally if you don't get professional help and do it right. The advice and guidelines listed throughout this book will make it easier.

By following these step-by-step directions, you will be gaining helpful information and arming yourself with a variety of valuable, practical tools. You will learn how to identify your articles; how to estimate their market value; how to find and use various available avenues for selling them; the mechanics of the selling process; and whether you would be well advised to consider the tax advantage of giving them as a donation to a worthy charity.

As you prepare yourself, be confident that you can make this transition comfortably and successfully by following the instructions provided herein. First, adopt a positive frame of mind.

*The Lion's Paw (above) and the
Australian Wentletrap (left)
are the kinds of shell treasures
worth searching and waiting
for — the ones Mrs. Lindbergh
called "significant."*

CHAPTER ONE

HOW TO TAKE A POSITIVE APPROACH

As you look over your inventory of "things" and plan this important task, maybe you can empathize with the collecting splurge of Anne Morrow Lindbergh at the seashore. She found herself so carried away with gathering up all the enchanting shells she saw in the sand at her feet that she was oblivious to the wonders and magic and vitality of the sea right in front of her eyes.

She said, finally:

"One cannot collect all the beautiful shells on the beach, only a few. And they are more beautiful if they are few. The collector walks with blinders on; he sees nothing but the prize. The acquisitive instinct is [usually] incompatible with true appreciation of beauty. We can have a surfeit of treasures, an excess of shells . . . where one or two would be significant."

Much, much earlier, in the sixth century B.C. the Chinese philosopher Lao-Tzu was on target, saying, "He is rich who knows when he has enough."

Think about these quotes and the other highlighted references throughout the book during the course of this gear-shifting phase in your life.

As you tackle the nuts and bolts of your wrap-up job, the best, in fact, the only, point of view to adopt is that you are going to simplify your life and improve its quality. And, in the process, you can reap a fine bonus: You will find many of the possessions that you take for granted or dismiss as insignificant may, in fact, be worth a lot of money—more than you could ever imagine.

For example, that photograph gathering dust on grandpa's wall turns out to be a valuable Ansel Adams original! And among those dirty bottles thrown into a carton in the basement is an Avon NAAC Club bottle made in 1972, now worth hundreds of dollars. And among the Pez dispensers that your small son used to play with are a "Pear with Visor" worth $600 and a "Mary Poppins" model priced at $115.

So it behooves you to give careful thought to what should be done with those miscellaneous items you have accumulated. Especially, you will train yourself to resist the mistake all of us have made and deplored, namely, hastily and impulsively giving away or selling for next to nothing a rare antique or fine piece of art that could turn out to be quite valuable.

Find out exactly what you have and its current market value. Do careful research. Make an inventory. Keep detailed records. And, by all means, prepare four important lists:

- What to sell.
- What to give away to friends and relatives.
- What to donate to charity.
- What you *must* keep to the end of your days.

These lists are your road map. Use them all through your sorting and unloading journey.

It may help you get oriented if you go back in time and review what has been going on in your life. Early on you were preoccupied with certain imperatives:

- Getting an education.
- Choosing and preparing for a professional career, a trade, or a business.
- Starting a marriage and a family.
- Enhancing and indulging your chosen lifestyle.
- Getting caught up in the consumption mentality of our culture as you acquired more and more luxuries—high-style clothes, bigger cars, showier furniture, and a myriad of gadgets and fads of the moment.

Let us assume that, having amassed all these material things, you are now at a crossroads in your odyssey through life. This is a good time for some serious soul searching—an opportunity to take a careful look at the treasures and trivia you have been accumulating and to assess the drives that spurred you to collect and, more important, to cling to them.

You will be motivated in this self-analysis when you ask yourself if you want to unclutter your life and your overloaded and overtaxed mind, and answer "yes." Begin by defining your needs in this crucial period and in the future. The byword is "simplify." Free yourself of the pursuits, habits, and possessions that have bogged you down, worn you out, and trapped you in a mechanical, routine pattern of behavior.

You will feel much better and happier with a fresh, realistic, undemanding outlook.

This may be the first time you have needed to examine the influences that led you to more and more acquisitions and what meaning they now have. In the process, think about the major disruptions that you have had to deal with.

You may find it necessary to reorganize your lifestyle in midstream because of:

- An important career or employment change.
- A geographical relocation.
- A marital break-up.
- Long-term travel plans.
- A drastic change in your economic status (big monetary loss, big inheritance, or big new financial responsibilities).

Pop-up Pez candy dispensers hold their own as hot collectibles. These are high-demand models.

At the far end of the spectrum are the changes required later in life because of:

• Children leaving the nest.
• Lack of space or time for your collection.
• Spouse or parent going into a retirement or nursing home.
• Becoming widowed.
• A late-in-life remarriage or live-in partner.
• And/or many other situations you can surely think of.

As you adjust to your new status, you may find your surroundings cramped, or you may see articles and personal memorabilia that evoke emotional or painful memories. You look at objects that once represented pleasure and security and realize that they no longer have the same meaning.

Sometimes we read in the newspaper of a person who has been found deceased amid piles of old papers and magazines, bottles, string, rubber bands, and other trivia. The irony is that this individual, obsessed with hoarding such worthless things, had hidden away bank books and cash amounting to big numbers. The security that he saw in piles of litter was an illusion.

Very old straw baskets and utensils, slowly and carefully crafted by hand, express cultural creativity as imaginatively and sensitively as the familiar art forms of music, painting, sculpture, and literature. This bamtush-weave POMO basket made a hundred years ago is distinguished by its unconnected triangles at bottom center. (Courtesy National Museum of the American Indian, Smithsonian Institution.)

Two views of an antique German stein, inscribed "AUFDER ALM-DAISTESSCHON! - 875 Germany."

How much better if he had taken the money and bought himself some comfort and pleasure—or even better, donated it to a worthy, meaningful cause.

These preposterous but true incidents are documented examples of what some people do when impassioned by the collecting and hoarding mania.

It will help you to analyze your situation if you know the mental baggage attached to the things you are fussing over. You may be clinging to certain articles for reasons buried within your subconscious mind. For example, you have a fixation upon an intricate Native American straw basket but don't know why. But then you remember that your mother bought it on her honeymoon trip in New Mexico. Once the underlying causes of your mysterious attachments come to light, you can decide how valid they are and whether they continue to serve a purpose. Think about, for example:

• Emotional or sentimental attachment to certain inherited or impulsively acquired articles.

Ask yourself whether these items are still giving you pleasure, satisfaction, or fulfillment. If not, put them on your "Sell," "Donate," or "Give-away" list. Consider that by giving them now to close friends or relatives rather than bequeathing them, the recipients will value them as you do, and you will be here to witness and share in their pleasure.

• The "security" you attribute to and associate with a treasury of material articles and assets.

Acknowledge that true security lies within your mental and emotional health, not in the external world of possessions. This is not to discount the importance of goods and property in today's materialistic world, but rather to put them in perspective. Rest assured, you will breathe much freer when you unload the things, and thoughts, that have been smothering you.

• Loyalty to your children.

Resign yourself to the possibility that your children may not share your appreciation of all your treasures and will not want them. Find out which, if any, of your things they admire and hope to own. It will make you and them happy if you give them those special items now. If your son has always looked with yearning on that antique Mettlach beer stein of the "7th Regimental Guard," give it to him and enjoy the pleasure you see in his eyes. Put the rest on one of your two remaining lists: "Sell" or "Donate."

Lightening your load calls for some common sense procedures: authenticating, appraising, and setting a sales price; figuring out the techniques of selling, packing, insuring, and shipping; and obtaining professional and physical assistance as needed.

IF YOU ARE THE STEWARD, BUT NOT
THE OWNER, OF VALUABLES

The same advice and guidelines contained herein applies even if you are not the owner of the valuables in question. Instead, as the executor of an estate or as temporary custodian, you have control of and responsibility for such articles. In that capacity, you also need to know as much as possible about their qualities, authenticity, provenance, and monetary value. This information will stand you in good stead as you carry out your fiduciary duties and responsibilities.

*   *   *

As you go forward with this undertaking, keep up your enthusiasm and optimism, and look ahead to a new positive lease on life. If you list the necessary steps one by one and make use of the methods and options offered here, it will simplify (here's that good word again) your job. This book takes you by the hand and leads you carefully through every stage of the mish-mash of tasks that lie ahead. Another look at the Contents page will assure you that your questions and concerns are dealt with thoroughly and in detail.

For moral support and good counsel, consider the wise words of Henry David Thoreau and of other philosophers that appear throughout the book.

Thoreau repeatedly emphasized the virtue of "simplicity, simplicity, simplicity" as the theme of his thoughts, behavior, and writings. But do not misunderstand. He never suggests that we literally take to the woods (as he did), eschewing all luxuries and comforts; rather he advocates reducing our "game plan" of life to the basics as we perceive them, following the belief that a person is rich in proportion to the number of things which he can afford to leave alone.

This may be a good time to reflect upon the theory of transcendentalism, which Thoreau, Ralph Waldo Emerson, Nathaniel Hawthorne, and many other sages espoused. It is living the good life by transcending and surmounting the mundane experiences acquired through the physical senses, such as sorting and filing knowledge, and collecting possessions.

Now let us turn to that "best of life" that Robert Browning tells us lies ahead.

This rare, original mechanical bank, "Girl Skipping Rope," by J. E. Stevens is more than 100 years old. It has been appraised at $40,000.

CHAPTER TWO

HOW TO SPOT THE TREASURES AMONG THE TRIVIA

"This is the happiest of mortals for
he is above everything he possesses."
— *Candide*, by Voltaire
(Francis Marie Arouet)

Most of us are aware of the intrinsic and commercial value of an antique Chippendale sideboard, a fine silver candelabra, a Tiffany vase, an artistic old handmade quilt, a proof coin set, an elaborate Oriental rug, a vintage Swiss music box, and other precious heirlooms.

If you have or inherit such treasures, it is not likely that you will dispose of any of them without getting expert advice. Keep in mind, if you act carelessly and hastily, you could be making a costly, irreversible mistake.

However, you will be surprised to learn about the big prices being realized from certain of your possessions regarded as bric-a-brac or unimportant trinkets.

Leave no stone unturned as you explore your surroundings, and take a fresh look at your miscellaneous collected possessions. This message is as good counsel today as in the fourth century B.C. when the Oracle at Delphi revealed how to find a treasure that had been buried by Xerxes' general, Mardonius.

As you turn over the stones — that is, examining your closets, basement, and garage — you will find troves beyond your wildest dreams. Imagine this: Back in the corner of a closet shelf is a long-forgotten mechanical action bank

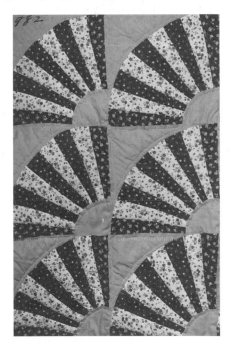

This is a handmade quilt of the traditional "Grandmother's Fan" pattern.

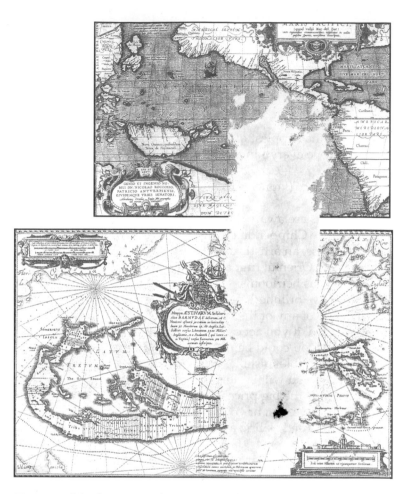

Two mythical maps—adventures in fantasyland. They contain misplaced, misshapen, and, yes, nonexistent oceans, continents, and boundaries. The viewer is amused by geographic and topographic inaccuracies, imaginary beasts and sea monsters, and strange embellishments.

in the form of a young girl skipping rope, all grimy and rusty with peeling paint. Worth approximately $40,000? Hard to believe, but, yes, "Girl Skipping Rope" is a vintage specimen appraised at that figure.

This discovery sends you on a search of your entire house, where you will notice, as if for the first time, many familiar, homey articles in your familiar, homey rooms and on the walls.

In the kitchen cupboard is a marigold colored glass vase that Grandpa brought home from a carnival long, long ago; a pair of platters decorated with artwork in blue that over-flowed or "bled" off the design; and a half dozen bowls referred to by Aunt Bess as "Depression" glass.

In the bottom drawer of a bedroom bureau is a little rug hand-hooked decades ago by a local skilled seamstress.

On top of a bookcase in your den is a bronze horse and rider wearing full Turkish military regalia.

A carton tossed into a corner of your basement contains an assortment of bottles: Avon, snuff, bitters, patent medicine, mineral water, ale, preserves, and ink.

On shelves and in display cabinets in your living room are a Black Forest beer stein with a Mettlach hallmark; a brass tower-shaped mantle clock; a pair of crystal candlesticks carrying the Hawkes mark; an inkwell with original stopper made by the Whitefriars company; and a well-hugged, slobbered over Teddy bear with a Steiff button in the ear.

On the wall of your son's room are pictures of a frontier saloon, an old mining scene, a turn-of-the-century Native American tribe, and a few mythical, fanciful antique maps.

Tucked away in a desk are a World War II ration book that Grandpa saved and some photographs that have the signatures of Jacob A. Riis, W. B. Post, and Mathew Brady.

A NEW APPRECIATION

This may come as a surprise and a revelation to you, but all of the above memorabilia and heirlooms are important, in demand, and valuable. For example, the platters in your cupboard turn out to be historical, so-called "flow blue" or "bleeding blue" china; the glass vase is authentic Carnival glass in a rare, sought-after color; and the bowls are genuine Depression glass specimens.

The Black Forest stein, the Hawkes crystal, and the Whitefriars inkwell are rare, precious antiques.

The historical pictures and maps have been kept in good condition and are valuable documentary memorabilia.

And the old photographs were determined to be genuine originals and are ardently sought after.

In the pages that follow, you will be told how to identify, authenticate, and evaluate these and other mementos and art-pieces that have been part of your daily life for many decades.

You may not be an art connoisseur or affluent dabbler in antiques, but right here in your modest home you have under your nose rare, unusual, yes, even precious antiques and memorabilia that you looked at time and again but did not really see, understand, or appreciate.

Following are just a few examples of the hundreds of article types that are in strong, continuing demand by collectors and experts and which are very highly valued. The prices shown are rough estimates or asking prices recorded in certain geographic areas at particular seasons or times of the year. Bear in mind the ongoing escalating trend that is sure to continue and even strengthen as time goes by.

BOTTLES, TINS, CONTAINERS

Some of these items are old, unique, and artistic enough to have acquired the status of antiques; they are categorized and evaluated accordingly. Bottles are grouped generally in four classifications:

1) Flasks and whiskey bottles: Hand-blown flasks made in the period between 1750 and 1860 are rare, artistic, and appraised at very high prices. The standard size has been and continues to be the pint. Vintage-style flasks are in such strong demand that they are continually being reproduced. These reproductions look very authentic, so the buyer should be on guard. Whiskey bottles became popular collectibles starting in the early 1800s with the introduction of unusual shapes, colors, and labels. Beninger and Booz are among the most-wanteds.

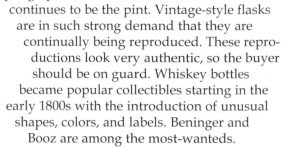

2) Bitters, the "medicine" of the last half of the nineteenth century, usually had a higher alcohol content than whiskey. It was the wonder drug of the times and was supposed to cure just about anything. It was also easier to tell your wife that the bitters was aiding your digestion than to admit that you were indulging in boozing, so bitters was a popular bestseller.

Collectors of bitters bottles look for the word "bitters" etched in the glass and a label extolling its curative virtues.

3) Figural bottles are the hundreds of types that have novel or unusual shapes or that look like recognizable persons, animals, or objects.

4) Household bottles are those used for milk, cosmetics, apothecary products, canning, and a large variety of utilitarian purposes.

Prices for very rare, unusual bottle or container specimens can range up to many thousands of dollars. For example, a Ross Excelsior, emerald green ink bottle has been listed at more than $7,000, and a Drakes Plantation bitters bottle at $5,800.

Tin candy boxes, biscuit tins, and cereal and other containers are highly collectible and worth up to hundreds of dollars. A one-pound Olympian coffee can has been offered at $550; a Pez dispenser featuring a clown with a yellow metal base at $300; and a Tobacco Girl Cigars tin at $2,275.

POLITICAL MEMORABILIA AND ARTIFACTS

These include campaign buttons, broadsides, posters, slogans, inauguration tickets and programs, banners, plates, and souvenir mugs. Items publicizing national presidential candidates are most wanted, but local politicians are popular in their own particular area of activity.

A certain avid history buff and scholar has collected more than 2,000 items designed and produced by proselytizing politicians in their attempts to capture the popular vote. He prizes above all his possessions a reverse painting on glass depicting George Washington's inauguration. Brass coat buttons commemorating Washington's election are very treasured as only a few hundred are believed to still exist. Washington is understood to have had a set of these interesting, unique buttons on the uniform he wore to his inauguration in 1789.

This Winston Churchill Toby character jug bears the Royal Doulton hallmark.

A political button featuring Republican candidates Harding, Coolidge, and Penrose in 1932 has carried a price tag of $6,200; a Woodrow Wilson Toby Jug, $1,950; and an 1872 doorstop of the figure of Horace Greeley, Liberal Democratic candidate, $2,500.

PHOTOGRAPHS AND PRINTS

Any photograph taken by a recognized, famous, creative photographer is a winner. In strong demand are photos by Ansel Adams, Margaret Bourke-White, and Man Ray, among others. Especially sought after are the works of Civil War photographer Mathew Brady, who himself or with his cameramen snapped thousands of wounded and dying soldiers on Civil War battlefields. Some of these vivid, poignant scenes are valued at many thousands of dollars.

"Young Girl and Infant," a limited edition fine print, 62/200, signed by artist Rafael Soyer.

Photographs of historical interest, such as people in vintage, old-fashioned clothes, turn-of-the-century Native Americans, frontier saloon scenes, paddlewheelers, old mining scenes, early architecture, etc., can be valuable even if taken by an unknown. A few years ago a flea market shopper paid $18 for seven old photographs of the U.S. Capitol and White House. They turned out to be the earliest recorded images of these buildings, and six of them were bought for $12,000.

Fine prints that are found to be genuine Audubon birds, A.B. Frost hunting scenes, Rafael Soyer paintings, or other rarities are worth thousands of dollars (see pp. 64-68 to learn about verifying what are represented as authentic prints).

POSTCARDS

Nearly everyone has a shoebox full of postcards being saved as sentimental keepsakes. Some of these small items, however, could be worth a lot of money.

I'M DO'N OK, HOW ARE YOU ?

The first U.S. picture postcard, printed by artist Charles Goldsmith, was released as a souvenir of the World's Columbian Exposition held in Chicago in 1893. Since then, they have been made of many types of materials—tree bark, leather, linen, silk, and various metals.

Serious postcard addicts search for those that depict actual locations and personalities, vintage apparel, historic modes of transportation, sports, political events, and advertising. The value of cards is determined by age, condition, subject matter, artistry, and rarity.

Cards signed by important artists of a time period can bring hundreds, even thousands, of dollars. Look for specimens displaying Christmas or Easter seals,

"KINGS OF THE BROAD HIGHWAY

Postcards showing World War II G.I.s.

TB or Red Cross insignia, or other commemorative stickers, which can add to their value.

Mechanicals (made with movable parts) command a premium if in good, working condition. For example, a donkey tail may wag or a head may nod. Especially high prices may be realized from fold-out, see-through ("hold to light") cards, and puzzle cards. Look at these astonishing prices:

An 1898 card titled "Waverly Cycles," which was illustrated by Czech artist Alphonse Mucha, was sold for $13,500; a card depicting a Socialist caravan horse and wagon, 1916 election, $3,600; and a card with a picture of an autographed Babe Ruth baseball and swing bat, $660.

KITCHENWARE

You probably have a gold mine right in your kitchen, pantry, or basement. If you cling to old-fashioned, nostalgic cooking and preserving devices, you most likely did not throw away that old, heavy rolling pin, butter mold, sad iron, ice cream machine, Griswold cast-iron baking pan, manual toaster, figural bottle opener, washboard, "piggin," or any of dozens of vintage kitchen tools and accessories. If you are ready to part with them, pay-off time is here.

Items that have great collector appeal and dollar value are those with the "country look" that have been crafted by hand, as distinguished from mass-produced factory items. Highly prized are the manually designed and fashioned items such as were forged in a blacksmith shop from the seventeenth to the early nineteenth century. Typically, they were devices used while preparing meals at the fireplace, such as trivets, iron forks, and metal pots and kettles.

Equipment that reflects changes and developments in home lifestyle is especially appreciated. In times gone by, food preparation, canning, preserving, etc., had to be done in the home with the help of seeders, egg beating devices, nutmeg graters, cherry stoners, nutcrackers, and other implements. The purpose of many "Rube Goldberg" monstrosities went by the board so long ago that they are enigmas and, as such, are in themselves a class of provocative, mystery collectibles.

Prints, boards, molds, and butter stamps were made to shape and decorate cakes, cookies, puddings, and other pretty edibles. Such food embellishers are highly collectible.

The most sought-after household devices are hand-operated utensils. In pre-electricity days, manual fruit juice extractors were in common use. The simplest juice reamers were earthenware, iron, or wooden squeezers that operated through means of a lever. Pressure applied to the lever crushed the fruit in a chamber that had holes

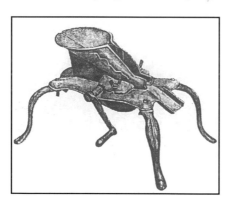

This cherry stoner, which can be screwed to a bench in the country kitchen, is adjustable for different sized stones. The cherries drop into a pan under the wheel, and the stones drop into a cup placed beneath the spout.

in the bottom, allowing the juice to flow through. More elaborate types had screw presses operated with a crank handle.

Other highly valued hand-operated items are washing machines and mangles, potato mashers, canister-type flour sifters, butter churns, coffee grinders, toasters, flat irons, wooden or metal ice boxes, and meat grinders or choppers.

If you were astute or sentimental enough to hoard any of these obsolete products, look at what you could get for them:

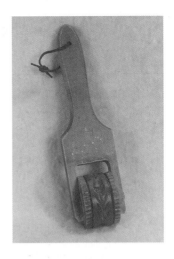

- Coffee roaster, Royal #4 . . . . $7,000

- Toaster, Blue Willow $2,200

An acorn and leaf design

- Pie crimper, whale ivory,
ca. 1850 . . . . $1,790

is the motif of this rotating butter stamp with handle. (Courtesy Archie's Studio, Vero Beach, Florida.)

- Waffle iron, Griswold No. 7 . . . . $750

- Egg beater, Quarter, German . . . $550

- Butter stamps . . . . up to several hundred dollars

BLUE JEANS

When Levi Strauss, a penniless young immigrant, peddled buttons, scissors, thread, and cloth in the San Francisco area to miners and ranchers during the Gold Rush, he founded an American institution and a thriving industry. The bolts of his canvas-like cloth used for tent making unexpectedly found a lucrative alternative market.

Prospectors and cowhands often complained about their thin cotton britches whose pockets, which had to carry gold ore if a prospector got lucky, "split right out." This problem inspired Strauss to make a rugged overall out of brown cotton "duck" that featured a tough, roomy pocket for carrying heavy stuff. Later he began using a sturdy fabric imported from France, which was called denim, from de Nimes, after the French town were this material was originally made.

These pants were later dubbed jeans, from *gene* (Genoa), identifying the cotton pants worn by Italian sailors.

During the past 120 years, jeans have attained the status of high fashion and have been steadily soaring in demand, thanks to the many additions and alterations Strauss introduced in response to consumer tastes and interests.

Many of us tossed our old, outgrown jeans into a closet but somehow could not take that final step to get rid of them. Those lucky ones and other enlightened collectors who may be casing thrift shops, garage and estate sales, and flea markets look for the following identifying features that enhance the value of collectible and marketable jeans:

- A ca. 1930 Levi jacket in good condition.

- A red tab on the back pocket of pants or front pocket of jacket; orange or white tabs are newer.

- A capital *E* on the tab that dates it pre-1971.

- A buckle on the back of pants or jacket.

- Inside rivets.

- The original button fly.

Old Levis in good condition that meet some of the above criteria are valued at $1,500 or more. A hot commodity in export markets, used jeans are graded by overall condition and the degree, uniformity, and quality of the fade.

The classic 501 is so popular that it boasts a special lexicon including Red Lines, Big Es, Hidden Rivets, and Indigo 501s.

A pair of mint condition 1928 Levis with rare vintage details such as exposed back pocket rivets and suspender buttons was recently purchased for $8,000.

And this may be an all-time high: A pair of pristine, never-worn, size 36, button fly dungarees made in 1929 received a bid of $30,000 from a Japanese businessman whose Tokyo shop sells old Levis. The owners turned down the offer and have secured the pants in a bank safety deposit box—to be used for their son's college education!

Whether bleached, indigo, 501s, or Big Es, jeans are worth big bucks in world markets. A pair of never-worn 1928 Levis with rare exposed back pocket rivets and suspender buttons received a bona fide offer of $8,000.

COSTUME JEWELRY AND FASHION ACCESSORIES

You may be pleasantly surprised to learn that your rhinestone necklace and your husband's discarded snap-together cufflinks that he tossed into a drawer may be worth a lot of money. The amount depends upon the craftsmanship, material, and signature, if any, of the designer/artisan. They could hold their own with many jewelry specimens made with precious metals and gemstones.

Examine your brooches, bracelets, rings, cufflinks, and other baubles for:

This brilliant brooch/necklace ensemble designed and fashioned by Hollycraft has stones carefully set with prongs.

• Artistry and detail of design.

• Quality of the metal and stones, even synthetics; Bakelite is rare and pricey.

• An incised ID signifying whether it is sterling, 14K or other amount of gold, or gold washed/plated; and other important information revealing age, rarity, etc.

• Whether the stones are set with prongs, which makes the piece more valuable, or glued in.

• The name of an important designer/manufacturer—Trifari, Corot, Warner, Monet, etc.

Don't overlook novelties, curiosities, or ethnographic items that might be highly valued and in strong demand. At a recent auction, a rare nineteenth-century Hawaiian necklace featuring ivory and finely woven hair brought $7,425, and a Crow Tribe choker with beaver teeth wire-wound opalescent beads, $5,500. And, incredible as it sounds, a Superman prize ring

Since the Endangered Species Act of 1973 restricted importation and sale of ivory items, such artifacts already in your possession have increased drastically in value. These two necklaces featuring ivory elephant art are very pricey.

distributed as a promotion in 1940 sold for $125,000 in 1992, and an Orphan Annie ring that was given away in 1941 as a premium for pennies and a cereal box top sold for $14,200 in 1993!

A novelty watch called "Swatch" has been taking collectordom by storm since its introduction in 1983. The thousands of models, designs, and themes enticing the buyer with marketing genius include a DAYGLO "Breakdance," a see-through "Jellyfish," and a chronometer named "Sex-Tease." Prices at issue range from a basic $50 up to and exceeding $1,618, the original cost of the platinum "Tresor Magique" when issued in 1993. It would be safe to say that anyone who bought a

Swatch watches have taken collectordom by storm since they debuted in 1983. Manufacturing and marketing hype captures an impassioned following who eagerly await each new release of the hundreds designed every year. Fanciful, outrageous, sexy, brilliantly colored models are named Metal Flash, Cherry Drops, Screw Driver, Sex-Tease, and Black Deco, for example. (Courtesy Archie's Studio, Vero Beach, Florida.)

Swatch, even one at the low end of the price scale, has a very good investment. Notice price examples of other costume jewelry:

- A pin of rhinestones and roseglass by Gripoix $230

- A Cartier scarf clip of white and black enamel and red coral border $1,430

- A Victorian lavaliere with two hanging garnets . . . $225

- An orange Bakelite bracelet with floral carving $85

Of course, provenance weighs heavily in arriving at current commercial value. Jackie O's pearl necklace, although made of pretty, well-matched, but only synthetic pearls, brought at auction $211,500, many times its already inflated estimated value of $4,700, only because it had belonged to and been worn by a celebrity (see pp. 70-72 for a discussion of provenance).

CUFFLINKS

In ancient times twigs were used to fasten shirt sleeves. Over the centuries, beautiful links were designed and fashioned. They ranged from simple primitive pieces carved by hand from bone, ivory, wood, and stone to rare "cuff pins" (ca. 1885), "wrap-around" closures, button closures, and "snappers."

A pair of Lalique links (ca. 1920) was recently appraised at $2,875, and onyx links depicting warriors' profiles at $605.

POCKETBOOKS AND COMPACTS

When leather disappeared for the duration during World War II, American ingenuity produced charming boxy creations from available substitute materials and synthetics. Some purses were works of art depicting scenery and animals or embellished with beads, sequins, and rhinestones. Such early pieces in good condition can be valued at upwards of several hundred dollars.

Other vintage bags made of fine mesh, lace, and the skins of endangered species are scarce and highly prized because they are fragile, and not many of them survived in passable condition.

Well-designed and executed metal compacts are also in strong demand, especially if they display artwork. Look for Art Deco designs, commemorative specimens from world fairs, expositions, and political events, and unusual features such as the incorporation of lipsticks and/or other fittings. Here are some documented prices:

Purses—Mesh, 14K gold, with sapphire-trimmed handle, $2,850; silver leather evening bag signed by Leiber, $325; black suede with faux amber frame, by Gucci, ca. 1930, $285; black patent leather clutch, by Leiber, $247; Lucite, by Rialto, marbled white, $75.

Compacts—George Jensen sterling silver, $375; bird shape, gold trim, signed "Dali," $250; green and gold cloisonné with attached lipstick on a chain, by Richard Hudnut, $240.

CORKSCREWS

A simple, mundane item found in the drawer of every-body's kitchen cabinet could turn out to be a highly valued collectible. Check yours out and see if you have an artistic, unusual, rare corkscrew coveted by serious addicts—and there are plenty ready to hand over big money.

These wacky little implements came into being centuries ago to resolve the long ongoing, ceremonial struggle between the oenophile (wine lover) and the cork. When wine was being transferred from wooden barrels to age and mellow in small stoneware or glass vessels, it wasn't stoppered and was prone to being damaged by insects, humidity, and air-borne impurities.

American figural corkscrew representing Senator Andrew Volstead, who initiated the Federal Prohibition Act in 1919.

In the mid-fifteenth century, a clever vintner fabricated a cork stopper that was cut off flush with the top of the vessel and sealed with wax. To remove the cork, a simple metal "worm" or screw was utilized with good results. By 1795, the first patent for a corkscrew was issued to the Rev. Samuel Henshaw of Birmingham, England. This device basically consisted of a handle shaft and screw, a mechanism that still does the job very well today.

Hundreds of devices have been concocted over the years to uncork bottles—as many utterly unusable as those that can do the job. Wine bottle corks must seal tightly into the bottle and must be moistened by the wine, whereupon they adhere by suction to the glass. The adhesion is so strong that to break it and extract the cork requires the force needed to lift a 100-pound bag of cement. This job must be completed smoothly, without breaking the bottle, splintering the cork, or contaminating the wine.

Mechanisms that have been invented to exert the necessary force were in the form of levers, curved gears, screw devices, or rack and pinion gears. A simple, reliable design is the popular Magic Lever Cork Drawer, which inserts the screw as

gears raise the lever; depressing the lever smoothly lifts the cork out.

Antiquity, precise workmanship, imaginative design, and precious materials are important attributes of a desirable corkscrew. All the better if it has a built-in cigar cutter, a knife, a buttonhook, or a brush for removing dust and cobwebs from very old bottles. An 1807 hallmarked silver model has a sheath, and, for a handle, a capped nutmeg holder and grater to make mulled wine.

A Thomason-type model has a brush and a decorated metal barrel.

One passionate collector got the bug when he bought three rusty corkscrews for $5 back in 1976. Now he has 1,100 specimens worth thousands of dollars. One of his most treasured favorites is an original Henshaw worth about $7,500. This ardent aficionado says, "The scholarship of corkscrews is a lot of fun." He admits to being captivated by the collecting craze and the technology and mechanics of the product.

A rare, steel two-pillar model patented by Scrope Shrapnel, son of the British general who invented the artillery shell, recently brought $5,000 in a Christie's London auction.

There are plenty of modestly priced specimens out there. An original "Naughty Nineties" model made of celluloid and nickel silver was offered for $300; a little tooled brass "Lady's Leg," $150; a Valezine aluminum with threaded barrel, $120; and a Willett's nickel-plated "Surprise" with rotating frame, $70.

Advertising corkscrew with aluminum handle and shaft. Italy, Art Deco period.

Corkscrew cast in silver-plated metal with decorated handle and shaft. France, nineteenth century.

A rare, lacquer-decorated Thomason-type corkscrew, England, nineteenth century. (Sir Edward Thomason [1769-1849] patented the double-action or telescopic model in 1802.)

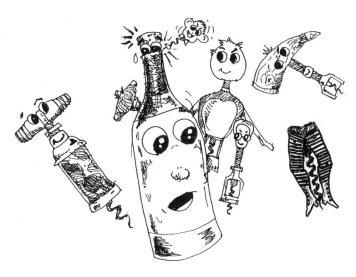

BOOKS

The value of a book is measured by rarity, condition, age, and popularity. As for age, some books written during the past thirty years can be worth far more than the average 200-year-old ones; it all depends on author and subject matter. Other important criteria are whether it has the original dust jacket intact, who owned it, if it has a bookplate or signature, who printed it, and its artwork and graphics.

First editions of important books command a premium. Look at the copyright page to see if it contains the notice "First Edition" and confirm that the date on the title page agrees with the copyright date.

In continuing high demand are old cookbooks, medicine books, and books about sports, decorating, horticulture, early science, and art. Special wanteds are very early children's books and artistically illustrated books.

Unusual photographs, engravings, or other attractive embellishments are great value enhancers. But often the pictures are worth more out of the book than the book itself. That is why many nineteenth century books of flower and botanical prints have been taken apart and the pictures sold separately. Look for illustrations by Wallace Nutting, Maxfield Parrish, N. C. Wyeth, Rockwell Kent, Bessie Pease Gutmann, and Arthur Rackham.

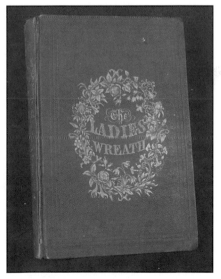

"The Ladies' Wreath," an illustrated annual dated 1849, contains many hand-colored botanical prints, pictures of historical sites and landmarks, and personal paintings. (Courtesy Archie's Studio, Vero Beach, Florida.)

High fashion frock and typical chemise-style under-garment as advertised in the Sears catalog of a century ago.

Covers are important. Good condition leather or gold decorated bindings, and unusual dust covers add value, as do fore-edge paintings (pictures on front edge of the page) and pop-up illustrations.

Of special interest are old mail-order catalogs. It has been said that the Sears Roebuck catalog was one of the only two books read by many Americans—the Bible ministering to the soul and the Sears catalog supplying every material necessity and luxury. Now that the Sears catalog has been consigned to history (as of February 1993), its requiem should memorialize the opportunity it gave rural America to obtain every imaginable product from Sears' horn of plenty. Notice some merchandise offered from 1897 on:

1897: Covered wagons, rifles, barbering accessories, buggy whips, and dubious medicinal aids including laudanum (opium).

1908: Wood stoves, ice boxes, frocks and trousseaus, A.J. Aubrey automatic engraved revolvers.

1910: Motor buggies.

1918: House kits with free building plans.

1927: C. Leo (Gabby) Hartnett catcher's mitts.

1931: Ultrasmart ladies' Silhouette foundation.

The catalog taught some Americans to read, and it set style trends for fashion conscious clothes buyers. And, having once advertised "the finest DeLuxe silk toilet paper," the catalog itself was toilet paper in many an outhouse.

What all this should do is give you an idea of America's materialistic culture, and its drastic changes, from the turn of the century to now. Above all, it positively indicates that this type of book can only go up, up, up in value. If you saved a Sears catalog (the older the better) or Montgomery Ward and others for that matter, you have a good investment as well as a slice of history!

What a contrast: Compare our ancestors carefully studying and selecting tempting articles from a mail-order catalog with the modern couch potato cradling a touch-tone phone while watching the Home Shopping Network.

"I do not know any reading more easy, more fascinating, more delightful than a catalogue."
— *The Log*
Anatole France

TOOLS

There's no tool like an old tool. You are lucky and rightly proud if you have saved in your garage or basement old, well-coddled specimens of meticulous craftsmanship, good solid material, and nary a trace of plastic.

Many dedicated tool collectors do not use their treasured prizes. They probably would be intrigued with the novelty of a fascinating rare folding rule, a French bow drill that is "played" like a violin, or a double claw no-faced hammer. They become inspired by the search, the discovery, and the appreciation of hand-fashioned, primitive implements of manual labor — irreplaceable, immortal relics of bygone, pre-plastic, pre-assembly line creativity.

A macabre side of the mania for acquiring ancient tools is demonstrated in the dispatch with which new widows are hustled by the dear departed's erstwhile buddies. One collector said that "Jim" wasn't even buried before a member of the local tool collector's club rushed over to help the bereaved widow dispose of all that "stuff." Of course he would relieve her of this and that and, out of the goodness of his heart, give her more money than it was worth. Fortunately, this widow

Four views of a rare, antique Bemis and Call Combination wrench, a pioneer of its class, highly prized by its owner/collector. The first wrenches were used during the heat of battle to twist bars out of castle windows. Later innovations were designed to bolt together parts of wagons and boats, even stone-throwing war machines.

was not naive and made it her business to seek expert advice before parting with anything.

Here is a humorous true tool story to cut your teeth on (yes, pun intended):

A Vero Beach, Florida, thrift shop received a donation of a quirky pile of pipes and metal. The shop managers assembled the mysterious motley elements into a composite structure and still did not know what they had. One of the metal posts was inscribed "horizontal condyl indication," which the dictionary defined as a "rounded process at the end of a bone, forming a ball-and-socket joint with the hollow part of another bone."

The curiosity was displayed in the store window and a prize offered to the first person to identify it.

Well, a local dentist claimed the prize. He said the tool was an articulator used for making dentures. It was of World War II vintage. Although a long time had passed and changes made since this old specimen was built, its function remains the same: to simulate an individual's jaw movement so that dentures can be properly tailored to fit each mouth, as no two bites are alike. So chew on that!

Old tools can be very valuable, as for example:

- A bed rope wrench, nineteenth century $4,000

- An ax, red goose on blade and handle $1,500

- Calipers, log, by Wm. Greenleaf $770

- A plane, Stanley, A78, Duplex Fillister $440

- A double-barreled cherry pitter $70

- A horse hoof trimmer $50

TOYS, GAMES, MARBLES, COMIC BOOKS, ETC.

It is not possible, in the scope of this overview, to even scratch the surface of the wide range of children's (and often adults') playthings that overrun the average home. But it would be wise to learn some basics about these captivating articles and how valuable they are in today's marketplace.

And, let us hope that you do not innocently repeat that unspeakable crime committed by a super-neat housewife (a friend of the author) when her daughter went off to college. She gathered up all those unsightly comic books that had been underfoot over the years and threw them out. What she threw away was in effect thousands of dollars, and, in the process, she incurred the wrath of a daughter!

Following is just an indication of the kinds of children's treasures that are in strong, ever-growing demand by members of the antique/collectible community. It cannot by any means cover the entire gamut but should at least alert you to the importance of evaluating every single one of the toys and cherishables that your children cling to before you part with them.

Let us start with that quintessential treasure, beloved by adults, even males, as well as children, namely —

DOLLS

Countless reference books have been written about hundreds of doll types that have been made, adored, and played with over the ages, even in prehistoric times. There is even a whole lexicon called "Doll Talk" used by dealers, experts, and collectors to enable them to describe and communicate about the subject.

For your purposes, it would be helpful to take a look at the dolls you have acquired and review a tiny representative sample. Of the U.S.-made dolls that are high-priced and in great demand, Barbies, with their fantastic wardrobes, equipment, accessories, and jewelry, are probably the most popular. They have held a strong, loyal following for decades, and their prices climb steadily. Trailing not too far behind are Madame Alexanders, Kewpies, Effanbees, Kestners, and other less-known but very well-made, desirable models.

Far outshining U.S. dolls in terms of artistry and prestige are antique imports, especially the Rolls Royces of dolldom, the Brus and Jumeaus from France; Simon and Halberg from Germany; and Steiner from Germany and France. Specimens in good condition are valued in the range of many thousands of dollars.

Among a variety of dolls and figures collected and prized by boys are G.I. Joes and Emmett Kelly clowns.

To identify your doll, look for the manufacturer's name under the hair at the back of the neck or on an attached tag. Be sure to keep the original box in good condition. A very important selling advantage is MIB (Mint in Box), even to the extent of doubling the price.

Another category of dolls to consider is paper dolls. Surprisingly enough, these delicate playthings have hefty price tags if in unpunched or uncut condition.

Emmett Kelly was a world famous melancholy clown and creator of the nostalgic hobo Weary Willie. Kelly was a master of pantomime whose sad demeanor and comical antics made us all laugh. Emmett Kelly dolls and figurines are in great demand and bring high prices.

Here are a few representative prices of certain doll types:

- Barbie, brunet, ponytail, 2nd issue, in box . . .$5,200

- Mme. Alexander, Jenny Lind, 1970, 21" $1,600

- Kewpie, bisque, signed "Rosie O'Neill," 12" $1,250

- Kestner, baby Hilda, blond mohair, antique gown, 19" $5,700

- Jumeau, Triste, long sad face, costume, 29" . . $17,000

- Bru, Brevetter, bisque, blue eyes, shaded lids, earrings, signed shoes, 19" $14,500

- G.I. Joe, British Commando, with accessories . . . $320

- Space Explorer, Moran, #103C, battery operated, in box $1,200

- *Gone with the Wind,* paper doll, uncut, 1940 . . . . . $275

- Aunt Jemima paper doll, Saalfield Publishing,
  6", 1910 . . . . $315

It is strongly advised that you research your dolls in one of the specialized reference books and in price guides.

TOY TRAINS

Before you start dismantling that elaborate rolling stock system that over a period of many years has been acquired, developed, added to, nurtured, and accessorized, consider the following:

1) Your collection of rare, unusual, finely crafted railroad cars and systems is probably worth a fortune. You would be well advised to do careful research and check out each and every car, locomotive, caboose, and accessory for manufacturer and current value.

2) Your little boy, now all grown up, may have been graduated to and is now a proud member of that elite Train Collectors Association. He would probably fight tooth and nail to resist parting with a single one of his precious stock.

3) Toy train railroading has become an institution, a way of live competing with golf, tennis, kayaking, and many other leisure time activities. The train buff stages a production, escaping his prosaic life for endless hours to become a powerful captain of industry with all kinds of rolling stock and maneuvers at his beck and call. This is not just a hobby. In the minds of its devotees, it is a philosophy, a religion, a calling.

All that having been said, if circumstances still compel you to dispose of these treasures, do it slowly and carefully.
Trains are identified by make, period of manufacture, and gauge. The Golden Age of Toy Trains dates from the 1920s, when the first mass-produced electric motor-powered trains were made, through the 1950s. Two gauges (i.e., the distance between the tracks' two outer rails) are the Standard, 2-1/8" width and the less expensive O Gauge—about half the size with a rail width of 1-1/4".

Today, many collectors choose the HO Gauge, a smaller version of O Gauge, with a track width of 5/8" and correspondingly smaller engines and cars. This more recent product allowed the building of elaborate "running layouts" in smaller space. According to recent estimates, active collectors of the HO Gauge outnumber all others combined.

The train's condition is of paramount importance in estimating value; items in only fair shape (scratched, chipped, dented, or rusted) have little monetary worth.

This Lionel model No. 400A was built in the 1930s.

You probably already have reliable information about how much your trains are worth. Otherwise, until you steep yourself in all that deep research and learn how to calculate value and price trends, these typical recent market prices may help you appraise some of the pieces you have:

- Lionel Standard Gauge, No. 4 Engine, Rapid Transit, 1908-1913, 14" $7,475

- Pratt & Letchworth train, N.Y. Central & Hudson, ca. 1900, 60" $4,830

- American Flyer train set, #4687, President's Special Passenger, track, box, 1927 . . . . $3,400

- Lionel locomotive, 1912 . . . . $2,970

- Freight train, Hiawatha, No. 757W $2,310

- Ives O Gauge, Limited Vestibule Express Set . . . $1,870

- Buddy L Caboose No. 1001 . . . . $935

MARBLES

Have you lost your marbles? Hurry and look for them in that long forgotten cigar box containing your childhood treasures. You may luck out and find a clambroth with red strands valued at $2,000. The marble buff's fascination with aggies, shooters, mibs, peewees, immies, and mariddles is addictive. This colorful terminology goes back to sixteenth century England, with later contributions from the sidewalks and backyards of American cities and villages.

Marbles have been played with all over the world for centuries. Ancient Egyptians and pre-Christian Romans enjoyed local versions of the game, and boys in the Middle Ages used the pastime as respite from the daily rigors of the classroom. The game was not just for children. Upper class adults in seventeenth century France enjoyed playing a marble contest called "bridge," and Abraham Lincoln reportedly was an expert at "old bowler," which requires precision shooting.

These glittery globes are seldom made of marble because other, more beautiful materials are available. Glass is most popular, followed by onyx, porcelain, agate, steel, limestone, and goldstone. The monetary value of collectible marbles is measured by age, material, craftsmanship, color, beauty, and design. Glass sulphides are highly prized and not meant to be used for play. They contain a three-dimensional figure embedded within the glass; if the figure is a train, ship, celebrity, or mythological beast, the value is much higher.

Alert: When cleaning your marbles, do not scrape away the pontil mark or stub that may be present on your specimen. This vestige, which remains at each pole after the marble is

A long-forgotten, hidden away cigar box filled with childhood treasures may contain rare, precious marbles.

formed, attests that it is handmade and, therefore, very desirable. Following is a list of prices realized for certain marble specimens:

- Sulphide containing a 4-colored hen $4,400

- Mica, turquoise oxblood $3,150

- Lutz, white polished onionskin $2,100

- Sulphide containing bust of Jenny Lind, the Swedish nightingale $1,600

TOPS

The whirling blend of colors flashing in a swiftly spinning top is a delight to charm children of all ages. This captivating sight is one reason that the top has been a popular plaything in every world culture for more than 2,000 years. Paintings and engravings on antique vases show children enjoying tops many centuries ago.

The varieties of styles, colors, materials, and techniques represented in top specimens range from simple spinners to porcelain figurals to lithographed tin hummers to twirlers to magnetics to gyroscopes. Grown-up boys can remember playing with a peg top, or a whip top, or a "draydel," or a teetotum.

In great demand by collectors are many styles of wooden tops made by imaginative cabinet artisans out of small scraps of exotic woods. Some are hollowed out or carved with small indentations or holes in such a pattern that a musical chord is produced by spinning the top. Some computer-age specimens—which might be equipped with microchips, sound generators, and tiny batteries—play songs when spun.

An ethnic top, called a draydel, in the shape of a cube that tapers to a point on the bottom and is spun by a peg protruding from its peak. Such tops can be made of silver, crystal, wood, or plastic.

45

At a recent auction, a top that was given away as a political promotion during the 1896 McKinley-Hobart presidential campaign brought $1,155. This was a spring-operated model with pictures of the candidates and a label reading, "Protection, Sound Money, Prosperity."

Here are some other prices that have been paid for various unusual tops:

- A French porcelain doll top with lace dress over tin, 3" $660

- A figural hummer, woman in hoop skirt, polychromed tin, 7" $468

- A gyro, painted tin man in green suit, top hat, 4-1/2" $341

COMIC BOOKS, GRAPHICS

Prices that have been realized in recent years for comic books are astronomical, and the uptrend is strong and steady. Notice the following prices paid for old, mint condition, first edition books:

- A 1938 *Action Comics #1*, featuring Superman . . $82,000

- A May 1939 *Detective Comics #27*, featuring the first appearance of Batman $68,500

- A 1962 *Amazing Fantasy #15*, depicting Spiderman $39,000

- A 1940 *Batman #1* $19,000

While looking over your store of comic books, hope that you have saved those with original cover graphics. Unbelievably high prices are commanded by the cover art-work for Prince Valiant, Little Nemo, Dick Tracy, and other popular heroes. A painting of *Fighting Men of Mars* by Frank Frazetta (who later illustrated for *Playboy* magazine) recently fetched $92,000, and a Carl Barks painting for an *Uncle Scrooge* cover, $112,500.

So let us hope you won't have to eat your heart out for the comic book treasures you once had.

ALL THE REST

Among the innumerable assorted collectibles that it was understandably not possible to include here, you should not fail to check these out before you let them go:

Lunchboxes	Mechanical banks	Watches
Pez dispensers	Railroad passes	Yo-yos
Gambling chips	Match boxes	Robots
Space memorabilia	Old valentines	Sheet music
Theater programs	Sports T-shirts	Cowboy gear
Napkin rings	Cameras	

You could probably add many more items to this list including new novelty items that are manufactured and introduced every day. Look them over, think them over, and cash them in if the time is ripe.

Some kinds of articles have traditionally been poor sellers, but—who knows?—even they may turn around in the course of time. They include sewing machines, foot warmers, flags, most old Bibles, and reference books.

Now that you have found a potential gold mine among your various possessions, you have work to do. You need to sort, identify, and classify all your antiques, artifacts, and collectibles. In the next chapter, you will get nice, easy lessons on how to do the job.

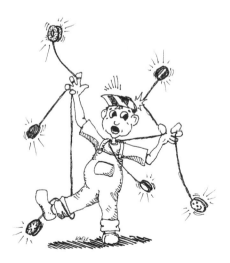

Artifacts depicting yo-yo type toys have been unearthed in centuries-old archaeological remains in China and Greece. The popularity of this toy stems not only from exciting competitive games but also its value as a tool for developing coordination skills.

CHAPTER THREE

HOW TO ANALYZE WHAT YOU HAVE

"I wiped away the weeds and foam
I fetched my sea-born treasures home
But the poor, unsightly, noisesome things
Had left their beauty on the shore
With the sun and the sand and the wild uproar"
—"Each and All"
by Ralph Waldo Emerson

So let us now take stock of the "sea-born" treasures we fetched home.

To undertake this important sorting, listing, and labeling task, the first step is to learn all you can about your accumulated possessions—their origin and history, authenticity, provenance, relevance and importance to the art/antique community, and, especially, their value baseline.

A. IDENTIFICATION

IS WHAT YOU SEE WHAT YOU HAVE?

Before attempting to understand and authenticate your possessions, you have to identify each separate article. For each article, get in the habit of using the term that is the common frame of reference understood by dealers, auctioneers, appraisers, and publishers of works about art, antiques, memorabilia, artifacts, and collectibles. This official "label" enables you to look up prices and other needed information in an efficient, time-effective manner. Without it, you are looking for information about something, but don't know exactly what it is called, so you may be led astray and find yourself dead-ended.

Libraries and bookstores are filled with periodicals, scholarly texts, and reference works that discuss many general product types and classifications, such as:

Vintage furniture
American pottery
Swiss music boxes
Art glass
Lithographs
Bronzes
Clocks
Tintypes/Daguerreotypes

Samplers
Georgian silver
Paperweights
French porcelain
Netsukes and *inros*
Lighting devices

There are scores of authoritative works about these and many other products available to the researcher. Following are just a few varied examples:

Baccarat millefiori yellow mushroom overlay paperweight.

• *Art Pottery of the United States*, by Paul Evans, Feingold & Lewis, New York, New York.

• *Guide to Lace and Linens*, by Elizabeth M. Kurella, Antique Trader Books, Dubuque, Iowa.

• *500 Years of Golf Balls*, by John F. Hotchkiss with a foreword by Arnold Palmer, Antique Trader Books, Dubuque, Iowa.

A list of additional references is provided under "Further Reading," p. 171.

Literally hundreds of categories and sub-categories are encompassed within the following subject groups:

KITCHENWARE: food choppers and grinders, butter molds and irons, teapots, cookbooks, coffee grinders, toasters, woodenware (treenware).

FOLK ART: decoys, tramp art, whirligigs, weathervanes, Frakturs, trivets.

Drawing of a vintage sad iron.

SPORTS COLLECTIBLES: signed baseballs, official team T-shirts, game tickets, golf balls.

PETROLIANA: oil cans, gasoline advertising signs, old road maps, pumps.

OFFICE AND STORE EQUIPMENT: typewriters, adding machines, cash registers, lawyers' bookcases.

The possibilities are endless.

This preamble is intended to show that your possessions may not always be clearly defined or delineated. Therefore, you need an explanation of terminology to help you research your specific articles. So here it is:

To look up something according to its correct name or label means, for example, to search for your tiny Japanese carved ivory figure under *"netsuke"* or *"inro."* Your bowl could be listed under silver, pewter, toleware, porcelain, enamel, or other material; or, alternatively, under its style, such as cookie jar, oyster plate, shaving mug, "bride's basket," jardiniere, etc. Your glass vase might be found under art glass, Carnival glass, milk glass, Lalique, Waterford, cranberry, sandwich, and dozens of other possible nomenclatures. So to find your specific item requires some careful detective work.

Once you know the commonly used label, you have the key to help you do further research.

Before you go on, you may want to find out whether your artifact is an antique. Technically and legally, antiques are broadly defined by any of the following descriptions:

• Objects of ornamental character or educational or historic value produced 100 years before the current date.

• Recognized works of classical art.

• Collections illustrating development and progress of the arts.

• Creative original works in bronze, marble, porcelain, terra cotta, parian, pottery, etc.

• Rare, ancient, ethnical artifacts.

U. S. Customs interprets the 100-year time frame to mean (in the case of imported articles) that anything made 100 years before the date of importation is an antique. However, most of the antique dealer community has a looser interpretation and tends to include as antiques old (not necessarily 100 years old) articles that have inherent virtue, rarity, artistry, and beauty. In the field of furniture, however, some authorities say that only items made before 1830 are antiques.

Obviously, then, the term antique does not have a single, universally accepted definition.

A very old rare wrench with unusual curved handle.

NON-ANTIQUES

Besides traditional antiques and artpieces, we should notice a whole new body of articles that people are captivated by and are accumulating with great interest. These are destined to be the valued collectibles of the future.

Some of them, designated as "miscellany" by prestigious auction houses, are simply "campy" oddities of little intrinsic or aesthetic value that have captured the public fancy. Among them are Pez dispensers, pogs and slammers, McDonald's mementos (toys, hamburger wrappers, paper cups, etc.), political buttons, petroliana, and lunchboxes.

Others are becoming desirable, appreciated treasures because of their beauty, artistry, and, in many cases, mechanical ingenuity. In this category are corkscrews, whirligigs, tools and weaponry, tramp art, marbles, mechanical action banks, early electric fans, vintage coin-operated machines, weather vanes, and advertising creations.

A whole lexicon of terminology has developed in recent years for referring to non-antiques and collectibles. Here are some of the most commonly used general terms:

Ephemera: posters, broadsides, valentines, tickets, menus, Christmas cards, and other items that were designed for and originally intended to have only temporary or ad hoc interest.

Exonumia: tokens and coins other than government issue, namely medals, tokens, scrip, marked ingots, and even wooden nickels.

Horology: clocks, pocket and Swiss watches, musical automata, and barometers.

Juvenilia: dolls, dollhouses and furniture, toys, lead soldiers, trains, Teddy bears, and games.

Memorabilia: vintage souvenirs related to theater, sports, Hollywood, circus, and rock-and-roll, including autographs, programs, tickets to important events, and letters written by famous personalities.

Militaria: uniforms, ordnance, regalia, decorations, medals, sidearms, swords, insignia, rank patches, and rationing-related items.

Miniaturia: tiny reproductions of dishes, clocks, circus accessories, candlesticks, animals, shoes, furniture, stoves, and musical instruments.

Tramp art: articles fashioned by special carving and layering techniques from cigar boxes, wooden crates, and other discarded materials. Tramp art can be in the form of furniture, mirrors, lamps, plant stands, clothes trees, etc.

B. AUTHENTICATION

IS IT THE REAL THING?

To find out if your porcelain bowl, Hummel figurine, bronze ballerina, silver tankard, or crystal vase is a genuine original creation and not a reproduction requires a familiarity with authenticating methods. Many of you may have noticed that the first thing appraisers do when studying an artpiece is turn it over to see if there is a mark, called a "hallmark," on the bottom. The word "hallmark" comes from Goldsmith's Hall, in London, England, where gold and silver articles were assayed and stamped to attest to their purity. If the appraiser finds a hallmark (which is often absent, and, in that case, does not necessarily detract from an item's authenticity), it furnishes valuable identifying information. It provides such details as country of origin, manufacturer, age, history, material, model or pattern, and even the identity of the artist.

You may have taken an impetuous fancy to and bought a curious pewter vessel, a cut glass bowl, or a Royal Doulton Toby jug. Or perhaps among the household effects you inherited from Grandma a mysterious colorful porcelain urn has captured your interest. How do you find out what these objects really are? The hallmark is the key.

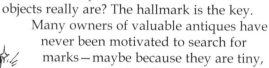

Many owners of valuable antiques have never been motivated to search for marks—maybe because they are tiny, often hidden, cryptic, and, in many cases, worn almost illegible. Yet these elusive signs are capable of revealing the whole fascinating story of the article's origin and worth.

These marks are not in and of themselves a guarantee that a particular article is positively a product of the manufacturer and/or the date indicated. However, when considered along with additional factors such as design, craftsmanship, material, and technique, they aid in identifying the piece and serve as a clue to its authenticity.

The amount, variety, and style of marks incised upon an object are endless. Interpreting them is a staggering proposition—a lifetime enterprise in itself. To attempt to review the entire gamut of hallmarks, trademarks, and touchmarks (i.e., identifying marks impressed on metal, usually pewter) in this kind of an overview is not possible. There are hundreds of separate volumes that list, illustrate, and explain the marks on every type of antique, artifact, and artpiece imaginable.

It is recommended that you spend a little time and effort researching some of the plentiful literature available about marks on your articles. Do this before you turn them over to an appraiser or buyer whose self-interest may override your personal needs and concerns. You have free access to plenty of resources in the library, bookstore, periodicals, the computer, and the expertise that dwells within museums, art galleries, universities, and historical societies (see Further Reading, p. 171).

In the meantime, practice examining and studying the bottom of your article to find and, if you are lucky, figure out the mysterious shapes and squiggles incised thereon.

FURNITURE

Many of you who have bought, inherited, or have an interest in authentic antique furniture are probably well aware of their attributes and have documentation of their age, period style, material, manufacturer, and even approximate monetary value. If you are in doubt, do some research before you dispose of a single piece. You would be well advised to consult a specialist in vintage furniture because it is a tricky area beset with reproductions, and you need professional expertise to help you verify what you have.

Aside from very old period furniture, you should be aware of more recent, humble looking under-rated furniture types that may have been in your home for some time but were relegated to second-class status. Certain tables, sideboards, mirrors, chairs, footstools, and settles (long, high-backed benches with arms) made by the following designers/manufacturers have been valued at prices ranging up to and over $10,000:

Heywood Wakefield	Gustav Stickley
Sunderland	Eames
Belter	Eastlake
Noguchi	

Shaker: You may have some of these unique furniture pieces and are not aware that they may be original, important, rare specimens. Shaker home furnishings and accessories constitute an inspired class of craftsmanship worthy of special attention and commentary.

What is their claim to fame? An impressive one, to be sure. Their legacy shines in the products of diligent, talented hands, created in compliance with the dictates of Shaker founder Mother Ann Lee. Her instructions were to craft objects that are "plain and simple . . . unembellished by any superfluities that add nothing to their goodness and durability." The work was done not by clumsy amateurs or casual dilettantes, but by skilled artisans who strived passionately to make every piece they fashioned a masterpiece of precise purpose and perfection.

By eliminating all decoration, stylization, and fanciful carving, they distilled the design of a chair, table, cupboard, desk, or washstand to its essence — to its purest and most basic form. These stark pieces are appreciated and widely coveted as classic creations.

In addition to furniture, the Shakers made many other utilitarian articles including candlestands, measuring tools, oval boxes, pegboards, and trays.

Because they are so deceptively simple with no fretwork, ornamentation, or intricate joinings to imitate, Shaker pieces are relatively easy to copy, and there are many reproductions on the market. If you want to authenticate your seemingly genuine piece, consult a museum curator or a bona fide expert specializing in Shaker.

You will be surprised to learn that a Shaker chest of drawers with original barn-red paint finish was sold for $15,000; a handcrafted clock for $165,000; and a cupboard for $200,000. In 1990, Oprah Winfrey paid $220,000 for a pine work counter, at that time a record price for a single Shaker item.

Wicker: This woven fiber stock, long considered of minor importance compared with more popular woods and furniture materials, is only recently becoming appreciated as a high-quality base material for artistic, even glamorous, furniture. In the early Victorian era, it was deemed good enough for only lawn, porch, and summer cottage decor. But during the 1880s, it captured public interest and began to be used for indoor furniture, street car seats, and even in hearse manufacture.

You may ask what there is about wicker that makes it an unusually desirable material for manufacturing certain types of furniture. In the late nineteenth century craftsmen discovered that melding the outer and inner bark of rattan with its flexible core fiber enabled them to make ornate, imaginative pieces with flexible lines and fancy curlicues. Early Victorian furniture featured wooden bead designs and decorations, undulating arches, and swirls thanks to the flexible nature of wicker.

An old wicker arm chair made of natural, unpainted cane.

When rattan became scarce starting in the late 1920s, fiber rush was used instead, and the furniture was no longer made by hand but by machine. Wicker fell into disfavor because it was not hand-crafted with natural materials as it used to be.

Nowadays, authentic Victorian pieces and Art Deco designs that had been introduced in the 1920s are in strong demand. The experts say "Get tough" when examining and assessing a wicker item. Twist it, shake it, turn it over. Examine it underneath. Check the paint; if you find clumps of paint in the weave, it means the paint was probably applied with a brush—taboo for wicker. In fact, painting wicker at all is a bad idea. The natural finish or a fine stain is much more authentic, attractive, and desirable.

So look with renewed interest and appreciation upon your old wicker furniture and accessories. They could be rare, highly valued examples of a nostalgic, bygone era. Do not part with them without careful research and evaluation.

POTTERY AND PORCELAIN

Many articles are simply called china or pottery but could more specifically be referred to as Delft, majolica, ironstone, bone china, hard or soft paste porcelain, lusterware, Belleek, Staffordshire, spatterware, biscuit ware, earthenware, and

Belleek porcelain: "A" is a Rathmore oval basket priced at more than $7,000; "B" is a Blackberry Basket, a rare high-priced design, discontinued and no longer available.

many more names. Some of the terms indicate the material of which the item is composed. Some are identified by the name of the manufacturer, e.g., Spode or Wedgwood. Some refer to the style or embellishments. Others allude to the unique color or glaze effect. And still other names suggest the use or purpose of the item, e.g., Mettlach beer stein or moustache cup.

As you use this book, you are better off not letting all this fancy terminology bewilder and sidetrack you. Stick with your goal of identifying and authenticating the particular item you have, whatever its technical name. Make good use of the hallmarks and other stamps, seals, and marks that help to establish your item's identity and legitimacy.

On ceramics and porcelains there are countless varieties of marks in the form of anchors, crossed swords, castles, flowers, coats of arms, etc. (see p. 54 for a discussion of marks).

Look at the bottom of your plate or bowl or vase. The first thing you may notice is the country of origin, which is a clue to its age. The U.S. Government passed the McKinley Tariff Act in 1891, requiring that the name of the country of origin appear on each piece imported into the United States.

If the name "England," for example, appears, it means that the article was made after 1891 (but possibly as early as 1887 if the manufacturer customarily had so marked its output). The words "Made in England" or another country were used for pieces made after 1914. Other date systems and marks may have been used for antiques or unique, possibly commissioned artwork.

Very old, intricately hand-fashioned and decorated Mexican sterling necklace.

In conformity with the McKinley Act, goods imported from Japan during 1891-1941 were labeled *"Nippon,"* which means Japan. After 1921, the law required that merchandise bearing only the catch-all term *"Nippon"* could not be distributed within the United States. To qualify for importation, the inscribing of a trademark began (such as an *"M"* in a wreath for Morimura).

SILVER

Among silver artisans, the United Kingdom's world renowned system of hallmarking, which has not changed in principle since the Middle Ages, is the accepted "bible" for assessing silver. Although even in England marks have been tantalizingly distorted by time and even by deliberate forgery, the law put in place centuries ago by London goldsmiths and still strictly enforced requires every piece of silver to be examined in an assay office. It is checked for its alloy content and either punch-marked (embossed with a figured punch or die) as approved, or it is rejected and broken up. Provincial assay offices may have their own distinguishing marks, often adapted from the town's or city's coat of arms.

There are countless identifying marks on silver. A rather well-known English mark is a lion, which means solid. The head of a king or queen means English made during the reign of the pictured monarch. Even if you do not recognize the monarch, you may have learned through your research that both King Georges (III and IV) faced to the right and Queen Victoria to the left.

This antique silver on copper Sheffield pitcher has fine contours and intricately detailed artwork in high relief.

An unusual silver Victorian bowl with reticulated lid retains much of its fine engraved artwork.

By studying available reference works on silver, you will learn the meanings of other signs: The letter gives the exact year of manufacture; a mark with several letters would probably be the maker's initials; a leopard's head means made in London; a thistle refers to Edinburgh; a harp, Ireland, and so on.

If the piece has only initials or a name on the bottom, it is probably American; silversmiths working during the Victorian era sometimes used a more personalized ID mark. For example, they would design a pseudo hallmark such as an eagle's head, a hand, a star, or a cartouche to convey the idea that the silver was the same quality as similarly marked English wares.

American solid silver bears the word "sterling," "coin," or the number "925," and plated can be identified by the words "triple," "quadruple," "Al," or "plate."

Old, rare Sheffield ware made in Sheffield, England, in the eighteenth century is very desirable but hard to authenticate. This is hand-rolled, silver-plated copper. What is often represented as Sheffield is newer silver plate marked with various combinations of shields, designs, and names, and/or the letters EPNS (Electroplated Nickel Silver) or EPWM (Electroplated White Metal).

There are numerous names or designations misleading one to believe that a non-silver article is silver:

"BRAZIL SILVER" is nickel.

"AFRICAN SILVER" is a type of English plate.

"OREGON SILVER" is a trade name for silver-plated ware made in England about 1880.

"SIBERIAN SILVER" is a type of silver-on-copper metal.

"GERMAN SILVER" is a clever German substitute for silver, made of nickel, copper, and zinc.

"WALDO" is a yellow colored metal tableware (see p. 54 for a discussion of marks and p. 171 for a Further Reading list.)

BRONZES

Look for the artist's signature or initials, foundry mark, patina, and other possible incised information.

Here are some examples:

A young ballerina: signed "Bessie Potter Vonnoh," foundry mark "OGWK Gorham," and a green-brown patina.

An Egyptian slave: set on a carved white stone base, signed "A. Wyon," dated 1912, and an olive patina.

"Robert Louis Stevenson" plaque: signed "Augustus Saint-Gaudens," stamped "copyright by Augustus Saint-Gaudens, MDCCCXCIX," and a brown patina.

A primitive huntress: signed "Cumberworth," foundry mark "VITTOZ Bronzier," and a brown patina.

The author's pride and joy, a bronze ballerina she dubbed Isadora, has a fine original brownish patina. This gem was created by famous sculptress Bessie Potter Vonnoh in about 1896.

This bronze, created by French sculptor Charles Cumberworth in the early 1800s, depicts an ancient primitive huntress with an infant slung on her back. Fine, intricate details are seen through its gleaming patina.

GLASS

The most beautiful and precious U.S.-made glass articles and the easiest to identify are the iridescent artpieces made in the period between 1894 and 1935 by Louis Comfort Tiffany and Frederick Carder. Tiffany usually signed his creations with the name "Tiffany," the initials "L.C.T.," or the word "Favriles." Carder artpieces were marked "Aurene," "Steuben," or with the signature "Frederick Carder."

Cut glass, especially of the "brilliant" period starting in 1880, is highly esteemed and treasured. Feel the edges of the design. It is easily recognized by the sharp edges of the incised design and by its heavy weight. It is also distinguished by its clear musical tone when tapped with a finger. Thanks to its many facets, it sparkles.

Only about 10 percent of all the cut glass manufactured was marked. Signed, marked pieces are not necessarily better than good unsigned ones, but, as is the case with most antiques, collectors place an extra value on the signed piece because it lends prestige and aids in identifying and dating it.

Paperweights: Any discussion of collector glass is duty bound to include information about paperweights. These exquisite pieces officially debuted with the creations of French manufacturers Baccarat, St. Louis, and Clichy in the early 1800s. However, beautiful globes of the millefiori (thousand flowers) design were unearthed in Pompeiian and Etruscan tombs more than a century earlier, and the technique used in their manufacture was detected in certain artifacts that had been made in the first century B.C.

A mint condition Tiffany iridescent gold, flared top footed salt is signed "LCT."

Paperweights and related, similarly constructed artpieces (scent bottles, flasks, vases, etc.) were regarded as "miraculous" considering the endless patience, skill, and supreme artistry that went into them:

• Preparation of the molten glass to achieve the unique lustrous softness of the crystal (a quality never since duplicated).

The St. Louis Marbrie paperweight has dark blue and chartreuse loops against a snow-white background. Distribution in the United States was limited to a total of 250.

• The blowing, building, and delicate drawing of the colored canes or fused glass rods.

• And the painstaking molding and sculpting of the entrapped glass and of the enamel flowers, fruits, butterflies, snakes, and animals shining through.

Each specimen is a unique masterpiece, so reproductions are uncommon. However, certain factories had lax standards and allowed their craftsmen to attempt forgeries. For example, Isaac Jacobs of the English Bristol Works produced imitations of Venetian glass, and Nailsea forgeries made in Birmingham were artificially aged by using acids. Notice the illustration on p. 75, in the "Fakes and Reproductions" section, depicting a weight identified as a fake made in Bristol; it gives itself away by a conspicuous date in the center. The authentic French date was very tiny and set in a subtle, hard-to-find position.

The Baccarat special millefiori (thousand flowers) paperweight.

Whatever reproductions make it through the assembly line are easily detected as blatantly inferior to the superlative qualities of original, imaginative creations—true works of art and a discriminating collector's passion.

It's hard to imagine, but these jewels were once intended for the mundane purpose of holding papers down!

An exquisitely illustrated book containing valuable information in layman's terms is:

> *Old Glass Paperweights*
> by Evelyn H. Bergstrom
> Crown Publishers, Inc.
> New York, New York

A word of warning: Almost every known type of art glass—blown, molded, pressed, colored, decorated, iridescent—has been cleverly reproduced for many years. These fakes were often made from the saved or unearthed original molds, using modern glass, which makes it well-nigh impossible to distinguish the original first casting from the reproduction. It takes a knowledgeable and experienced expert to tell the difference.

FINE PRINTS

A priceless painting by a world-famous artist is not likely to be found in the average modest home. However, any one of us may have inherited or acquired excellent valuable art at an affordable price. Check out that print hanging on your wall, which may happily turn out to be not a reproduction made by a photomechanical process or an out-and-out forgery, but a desirable, fine authentic print.

Modern Prints: Most of the activity in the print market today revolves around modern and contemporary works, so this discussion will start with the products of recent times. Current standards for judging the artistic virtu of prints focus on how much and in what way the artist was involved in the process that produces prints from his creation. This guideline was developed to resolve long-standing confusion and conflicting interpretations of what constitutes a fine print. Basically, what it does is replace the bandied about term "originality" which has no explicit definition in the context of modern printmaking.

Involvement by the artist is measured according to any of the following categories. The list does not purport to evaluate the merit of a print or to indicate poorly executed ones or fakes. It intends to serve only as a guideline for the layman to figure out what he has.

Before reviewing the list, one needs to understand the meaning of the term matrix. It refers to the medium in which the image to be printed is prepared. It can be a wood block or linoleum block (for relief prints), a metal plate (for engravings and etchings, or intaglio prints), or a smooth stone (for lithographs). In other words, it is any type of surface from which a true copy can be printed. Think of fingerprints, car tires, and rubber stamps as examples of matrixes.

Here, then, is the list, numbered 1 through 7:

1) The artist alone prepares and creates the matrix.

2) The artist and collaborator(s) prepare and create the matrix. The collaborator usually contributes technical expertise or performs laborious, time-consuming, necessary tasks.

3) The artist does not work on the matrix. He provides a design to be copied and is critically involved in direction of the work, suggesting modifications, and approving the resulting matrix. The physical labor is performed by a collaborator.

4) The artist has no meaningful involvement in the matrix production. In this case, the artist or his agent supplies a printmaker with a

Original painting of a Siamese cat KIM signed by KWO.

design to be printed as faithful to the master as the chosen print medium will allow.

5) The artist or his agent authorizes the reproduction of one of his/her existing works.

6) A reproduction is made without the permission of the artist.

7) A print is made from the primary matrix without the artist's authorization.

Old Masters: Until the middle of the nineteenth century, i.e., in pre-photomechanical times, all prints were made by various types of manual techniques, which imparted special craftsmanly qualities. Thus, printmaking during this period manifested an enormous diversity of artistic expressions.

Anne of Cleves, fourth wife of Henry VIII, was painted by Hans Holbein in the fifteenth century and is shown here as engraved in Mezzotint and printed in color in one printing by artist S. Arlent-Edwards. This is one of only 225 signed prints, after which the plate was destroyed.

For the earliest prints, often the roles of the artist who invented the image and the collaborator who created the printing matrix overlapped and became obscured. This posed an attribution question in many cases for print students and collectors.

Another problem in dealing with very early prints was caused by posthumous impressions thrown upon the market; entrepreneurs often purchased plates from estates of deceased artists and republished their prints under their own names. Those impressions are usually inferior to the ones taken originally by the artist: First, the plate was apt to be worn or damaged, resulting in a flawed product; secondly, the publisher often took the liberty of retouching the plate, thereby seriously compromising the primary intent of the artist. A case in point is the infamous reworking and reprinting of Rembrandt's plates far into the nineteenth century, drastically vitiating their originality.

By the middle of the nineteenth century, advances in photo-mechanical reproduction of images generated a flow of assembly-line simulations of prints and graphics. Whether the process is heliogravure or collotype, these are mechanical reproductions — photographic copies pure and simple.

Identifying Data: A signature on a document or print serves as a guarantee that the signer has inspected and approved the content. The earliest prints were not signed at all. Hand signing became customary during the second half of the nineteenth century. But there were so many variations and deviations in the signing methods that there is no standard to rely upon.

At the beginning of the twentieth century, prints usually contained the number of the print but no indication of the total in the edition. In about 1915, responding to public and professional demand, more and more editions were numbered as they are today, e.g., 1/100, 73/200, etc., showing both the sequential number of the print and the total number in the edition.

The subject of signatures, proofs, and editions is too complicated to present here with any degree of specificity. For advice and guidance in deciphering and interpreting the signatures, numbers, inscriptions, codes, or other data on your print, write to:

The International Fine Print
Dealers Association
485 Madison Ave., 15th floor
New York, NY 10022

They will be glad to refer you to member experts near you who specialize in your type of print.

The foregoing segment on authentication provides an overview of the various ways articles may be marked. It by no means purports to tell you everything about the science of detect-

The woodblock print originated in early eighteenth century Japan. Admirer James Michener said, "It is one of the most delightful art forms ever devised. Its colors are varied, its subject matter witty, its allurement infinite." This original woodblock was created in 1957 and signed by Unichi Hirotsuka.

ing the origin and identity of specific pieces of art. To learn how to spot, research, and trace important marks is an enormous, highly specialized process. But it is an essential first step to becoming secure in your knowledge of and ability to deal with your specific collections. Keep referring to authoritative works in bookstores, libraries, museums, and art galleries (see Further Reading, p. 171).

In your research, do not overlook historical and genealogical societies, major libraries, and museums as sources of specialized information about a full range of article types.

MUSEUMS

Even if budgetary and time stringencies limit their search time and personal attention, most museums and art galleries gladly provide resources to inform and educate you about your particular heirlooms and artifacts.

The principal service for the layman is in clearly attributed exhibits, catalogs, slides, and publications. Museum bulletins provide illustrated data on a wide range and variety of subjects. These are indexed in the museum's library and available in its files, even if not currently in print and on sale.

Many museums also offer high-caliber lectures by professionals on a variety of subjects and article categories.

HISTORICAL/ GENEALOGICAL SOCIETIES

These organizations are repositories of valuable information about your mystery heirloom or collectible. They can unearth and furnish you with important background data about its origin, age, artist, craftsman, and designer/manufacturer. And they can refer you to restoration and repair services.

Outstanding among such organizations is the Massachusetts Historical Society, which recently celebrated its 200th birthday. This storehouse of priceless documentary treasures cherishes among its prizes Paul Revere's own account of his midnight ride; the journal of John Winthrop, first governor of the Massachusetts Bay Colony; and the personal diary of Salem witch trial judge Samuel Sewell. It has a special, little-known historical gem: a daguerreotype of the disfigured hand of abolitionist Jonathan Walker, who was caught helping slaves to escape. The letters "S.S." (slave stealer) were branded in his palm.

Here are two addresses of historical societies and agencies:

Historical and Genealogical Societies
The U.S. Library of Congress
Jefferson Bldg. #244
Washington, D.C. 20540

The American Association for State and Local History
708 Berry Road
Nashville, TN 37204

(This resource provides data about preservation, restoration, and interpretation of historical artifacts, collections, genealogy, and historic sites. It publishes a list of 5,865 state and local historical agencies.)

LIBRARIES

Following are descriptions of two of the most important libraries in the United States where you can find every book, document, photograph, text, reference, and fact about your collectible, whatever it is. Your local municipal, branch, or university library probably already has or is gathering a respectable complement of similar resources. Meanwhile, these two giants are at your service: the Library of Congress and the New York Public Library.

1) Originally called the National Library of the United States, The Library of Congress was opened to the public in the early 1830s. Its first catalog of holdings, published in 1802, contained only 182 items.

Now it is the largest library in the world with more than 85 million items, including at last count:

• 20 million volumes and pamphlets
• 4 million maps and atlases
• 34 million manuscripts
• 10 million photographs, negatives, prints, and slides
• 6 million microfilms (microfiches) and flat transparencies.

The Library of Congress has a Telephone Reference Service and a Photo Duplication Service that will search out books, technical reports, maps, and photographic material and will provide photocopies of requested material for a nominal charge.

This Library does not undertake research on behalf of its patrons, but its Information Office will explain how one can utilize its various services.

Library of Congress
1st and Independence Ave., S.E.
Washington, DC 20450

2) A research library, museum, and archive, the New York Public Library has at least 6 million volumes and 12 million non-book materials, including manuscripts, maps, photographs, and prints. It has excellent special collections dealing with:

• performing and visual arts, ethnic subjects, humanities, and social studies
• science and technology
• patents
• rare books
• manuscripts

Personnel will undertake computer searches, photocopying, and research at a small charge.

The New York Public Library
Fifth Ave. and 42nd St.
New York, NY 10018

C. PROVENANCE

WHAT CELEBRITY OWNED IT?

You are likely to run across the word "provenance" with reference to antiques, art, and vintage furniture and jewelry. The term may sound mystifying, but it can be explained very simply.

In the case of an old painting, porcelain artpiece, or other creation or heirloom of reputation and importance, the seller will often indicate that "provenance" goes with it or is available or on record. This means that the article has a documented, verifiable history of ownership.

It is NOT a certification of authenticity, although the implication is that the more prestigious and famous the line of ownership, the more reliable its legitimacy. Sometimes the market value of the item stems only from the fame and status of the previous owner(s).

For example, a surge of interest in cookie jars was generated by the sudden death of artist Andy Warhol. A collection of his humdrum, inexpensive jars brought thousands of dollars at auction thanks to a spontaneous bidding frenzy—even though the jars had no artistic or intrinsic merit. Celebrity provenance and nothing else was the catalyst.

Provenance can be shown and accepted in various forms. It can be an original bill of sale; verifiable written notes on the back of a painting; a signed statement from a known previous owner; and other documentation. Even verbal hearsay is acceptable if it can be verified.

The influence of provenance upon an article's value can be demonstrated in unexpected ways. Here is an interesting example: An art buff on an impulse bought a portrait painted by a prominent local artist even though the eyes and mouth of the beautiful model had been badly scratched and mutilated. Of course, this damage presumably rendered the painting worthless.

Jackie O's faux pearl necklace: Provenance alone pumped up its price from an already inflated pre-sale estimate of $500-$700 to a whopping final bid of $211,500 at her estate auction.

But no, provenance came to the rescue. It turned out that the sitter had at one time been a favorite student of the artist. His wife found the painting in his studio and in a fit of jealous rage mutilated and discarded it, hoping that it and its history were gone forever. It survived. This dramatic incident, reliably verified, greatly enhanced the value of a far-less-than-mint work of art.

Provenance can turn out to be a fickle mistress. A price that was catalyzed to astronomical heights by the fame and popularity of the owner can just as suddenly plunge to deep depths if an owner fell into disfavor or oblivion.

Case in point: The upside—A necklace of Jackie O's faux pearls brought $211,500 at the April 1996 auction of her estate, far, far above the already inflated estimate of $500-700. That hysterical four-day event brought $34.5 million, seven times the pre-sale estate estimate of about $5 million. It was provenance at work!

At the other end of the phenomenon is the sad showing of the Duchess of Windsor's jewelry. At a 1987 auction of her collected pieces, a gold, diamond, and amethyst necklace fetched $605,000 after lively bidding. Two years later the same bauble was offered, but its price plummeted to $154,000. Bidders queried, "The Duchess of who?" Sic transit gloria . . .

Setting aside celebrity-inspired bubble and getting down to cases, the job of validating provenance is a laborious endeavor, an art not widely known or practiced. One of the few active specialists was Patrick Leperlier, who was hired by Christie's to probe Europe's ancient archives and verify ownership of certain art objects. His eagle eye, he reported, "recognized royal taste when photographs of two vases crossed my desk." He placed these swan-handled ewers at the gates of Marie Antoinette's palace in ca. 1783. She later sent them to a dealer for safekeeping before fleeing Versailles.

A novice would be at a loss to confirm provenance of artwork he owns. He can consult the catalogs published by auction houses, but the kind of documentation published there is purely statistical. It omits negatives surrounding the item, such as failure of the painting or vase to sell at a previous auction, the fact that a Nazi officer had stolen and stashed away the item, or any other dicey tidbit.

Good sources of provenance information are gradually becoming available to anyone interested and experienced enough to undertake computer research through network services.

D. CATALOGUES RAISONNÉS

RESEARCH THE "INSIDER" WAY

If you have a painting signed by Rafael Soyer, Salvador Dali, or Andy Warhol—or a bronze purported to be the work of Paul Manship or Malvina Hoffman, you may be able to find a catalogue raisonné listing and describing their work. Such a compilation is a very valuable authenticating aid that may be available in a fine arts bookstore or an auction gallery.

These resources are annotated, illustrated books listing the works of important artists, usually compiled by art historians, scholars, and curators. The thorough, relentless research pursued by these experts brings to light misapprehensions and errors even of recognized authorities.

For example, one of the earliest published catalogs of the works of Rembrandt van Rijn released in 1906 listed 558 works attributed to him. Dedicated art sleuths working on catalogues raisonnés have whittled the number of authentic pieces down to about 300. New York's prestigious Metropolitan Museum of Art once boasted forty-two Rembrandts in its collection. The number is now eighteen; the other twenty-four turned out to be fakes.

Catalogues raisonnés have been prepared on hundreds of artists, including Dali, Picasso, van Gogh, Rothko, and others of that caliber. But not all of these compilations are of comparable coverage. Sometimes authentic artworks are omitted, either through oversight or error. Subsequent research usually corrects such mistakes. For example, Vivian Endicott Barnett, whose first catalogue raisonné on the watercolors of Wassily Kandinsky was published in 1992, later found a previously unknown landscape by the artist that was brought to her by a collector. Its authenticity was verified by Kandinsky's handwriting on its back and also by tracing its provenance.

Currently in production are catalogues of Alexander Calder, Andy Warhol, Georgia O'Keefe, and Marsden Hartley, among others.

Although there is as yet no single directory of catalogues raisonnés, auction house specialists and knowledgeable dealers should be able to tell you if a particular one exists or is in the process of being developed.

E. FAKES AND REPRODUCTIONS

SPOT THAT FRAUD

In examining your stockpile of accumulated antiques and heirlooms, you should be alert to possible forgeries, shams, and other deceits in a seemingly original artifact. This is quite a challenge because the detecting of fraud has eluded the experts for centuries, and still does.

In the case of a fine piece of art glass, a porcelain or bronze figurine, an original print, or any article produced from a mold or matrix, you hope that what you have is the artwork emanating directly from the original casting. The output from that casting would have been limited to a small number of pieces, usually no more than a few hundred. To your dismay, your item could turn out to be a mass-produced copy worth very little.

The sad truth is that reproductions have long been and are still being made and thrown on the market as originals. A reputable dealer or distributor will specify that his merchandise is a recast, either from the original mold or a production run from a brand new mold exactly like the original.

Articles made after a long period of not being manufactured, even if produced from the original molds, are reproductions. However, they may often be represented by the manufacturer as early originals.

Reproductions have long posed a serious problem for art connoisseurs. Case in point: Glass manufacturers that have acquired a supply of old molds have the capability of reproducing fine early glass pieces. This practice will plague the antique business for years to come.

There was a time when honest manufacturers shunned and disclaimed any connection with reproductions. But the manufacture of such wares carried on secretly was a break in the dike that supported the traditional honor system. This encouraged many producers to join in the lucrative business of making and distributing reproductions that they passed off as originals.

Look for an imprint in the glass or porcelain article in the form of an initial or trademark identifying the manufacturer and signifying that the item is a reproduction. A few honorable producers do mark their output in this way, but do not expect the entire industry to voluntarily provide such an admission on their new wares that would negatively impact their sales.

Some responsible companies advertise forthrightly that they produce and sell "early American reproductions" or "antique or art glass in special new colors" or "reproductions of Frederic Remington western bronzes."

Goblets are a popular item that lends itself to reproduction, especially if it involves investment by the manufacturer in an expensive new designer mold because the consumers usually buy a set of eight or twelve pieces at a time.

Certain cagey producers comply with disclosure requirements by affixing a paper label to the article. Paper, of course, will not survive the first use and cleansing of the glass bowl or ceramic vase.

With reference to paintings and sculptures, fakes have been passed off as genuine for centuries. A popular story that makes the rounds repeatedly is that the artist Corot produced 1,000 paintings in his lifetime; of these, the yarn goes, 103,000 are in the United States and 30,000 in France!

From time immemorial, art frauds have been perpetrated — loose cannons running amok and rarely brought under control. The age-old art racket crops up wherever and whenever affluent people with leisure time and an appetite for "culture" seek an ego trip and are naive enough to be gulled.

For example, a statuette made in Egypt in the seventh century B.C. was designed in the style of the XII Dynasty of at least 1,000 years earlier. It was accepted as an authentic original without so much as a raised eyebrow by the sophisticated art experts. Thus, even the well-informed Egyptians of many centuries ago were taken advantage of by forgers exploiting human greed.

In ancient Rome as well, unscrupulous artists found a gold mine. Some of the Greeks who lived there were talented copyists who signed statues they made with the names of the famous Athenian sculptors Praxiteles or Myron, or their paintings with the name of the Greek artist Zeuxis.

But it was that mischievous kid Michelangelo who really misbehaved. As a youth during the Renaissance he sculpted an "antique" sleeping Cupid for his own amusement and then had the idea of offering it as a centuries old original to a dealer in Rome. He, in turn, easily palmed it off to

The English-made paperweight in this drawing gives itself away as a fake, a poor imitation of the fine French weights. It has a large date right in the center, contrasted with the French tradition of inserting tiny dates in hard-to-find locations.

Raffaello Riario, Cardinal of San Georgio, an avid antiquarian, for the astronomical price of 200 ducats.

In the twentieth century a super faker came along and carried off a phenomenal feat. Embittered when his painting talent and style were spurned by the art community and connoisseurs, Hans van Veegeren retaliated by painting six exceptionally fine works emulating the creativity of seventeenth century Dutch master Jan Vermeer. They brought more than $3 million, and for years one of these paintings hung in stately honor as a Vermeer original in the Boymans Museum in Rotterdam.

Such fakeries were rampant hundreds of years ago and have continued unabated to this day. In the past few decades, more than ever before, art forgery has flourished as an immensely profitable business. People are wealthy; more people can afford to buy fine art than in the past, and there simply is not enough available to meet demand.

The bogus art racket has shifted from the duplicating of traditional old masters, a difficult, time-consuming labor, to wholesale imitations of twentieth century artists including such favorites as Chagall, Picasso, Miro, Derain, Modigliani, and Matisse.

Not too long ago a reputable art dealer in New York City who should have known his stock in trade better staged an all-Modigliani show at his prestigious gallery. Connoisseurs who viewed the display rated the exhibition absolutely marvelous — observing that there wasn't one genuine Modigliani painting in the entire show.

Another shameful example relates to the art of Peter Karl Faberge, who designed and produced exquisite jewelry and artpieces, and is most noted for bejeweled imperial Russian Easter eggs. According to a New York dealer who specializes in the works of this designer, there is more artwork labeled Faberge in New York, Rome, Chicago, London, and Paris — in each of these cities — than he made in his entire career. Talented craftsmen would take a fine piece of jewelry, copy the Faberge hallmark, affix it to the piece, and multiply the price many times.

In addition to outright copying, various methods of tampering are practiced by unscrupulous fakers. For example, forgers sometimes cut an old silver hallmark out of a damaged or discarded piece and soldered it onto a new reproduction. Or clever craftsmen might take simple, classical eighteenth century artpieces and emboss nontypical ornaments and decorations on them to pass them off as novel, original art forms.

In recent decades, the popularity and exploding prices of Tiffany and other art glass creations spawned a huge business in forgeries and reproductions of Art Deco and Art Nouveau works. The fakes being produced were so beautifully and perfectly executed that to distinguish them from authentic original pieces in mint condition was well-nigh impossible.

Some such shams are entirely modern throughout, using new materials. Others incorporate some antique and some new glass. Many are assembled ("married"): for example, a new lamp shade might be put on an old base. Some enterprising forgers have acquired old Tiffany windows from dismantled churches and used the antique glass to fabricate many lighting devices and shades from large windows.

With all this chicanery going on, separating the genuine from the bogus is far beyond the capabilities of the layman. It is advisable to consult specialists and reputable, experienced professionals for assistance.

But even the pros are not 100 percent, absolutely infallible in their judgments and often differ among themselves when they study an artpiece. For example, an Art Nouveau expert at the prestigious Christie's auction house, after examining two lamps that had been identified in the auction catalog as fully signed Handel specimens, said they were not authentic originals but modern copies. When he was challenged by several dealers, he performed other tests including cutting into the copper on the inside of the shade to see if it had been attached with glue (which would indicate that it was probably old) or had a more recent adhesive backing to indicate that it was modern. At the same sale, Christie's withdrew its guarantee that a certain Tiffany Lotus lamp was genuine, because several dealers had insisted it was a fake, and the Art Deco expert himself could not confirm its pedigree. He had this to say: "Once a design has been questioned, that fact seems never to be forgotten, and its value definitely is lowered."

Here's a topper. An embarrassing boo-boo was made by the Grosvenor House Art and Antiques Fair in London in early 1996. It promised, "Every item . . . has been vetted (certified) for quality, condition, and authenticity." But when the Queen Mother's pair of Chinese porcelain cache-pots were exhibited, the vetters made a shameful discovery: The jardinieres turned out to be not from the Kangxi period (1662-1722) as claimed, but dated from the late nineteenth century. To add insult to injury, they were not Chinese but had been made in Paris. This fair was one of the highlights of the London art season. Its organizers covered their embarrassment by proclaiming that this discovery made the pots "even more interesting" but another source sneered, "That means they are nasty little fakes."

So, the inexperienced collector has to depend upon all the research and study resources available as well as, often, his own ESP and intuition. But he can learn a lot from hands-on practice and close observation. He can ask, for example:

Is the color of the glaze on that purportedly eighteenth century English bowl deep and intense enough, or is it a shallow, recent glaze applied to a blank?

Are the scratches on the item consistent with the two centuries of age and wear claimed for it, or do they look contrived and similar, as if all occurring at the same time?

Was the signature on a Hofman painting dated 1934 done with ballpoint or felt-tip pen? These types of pens were not invented until a decade later.

ADMIRABLE FAKES

This segment about fakes and reproductions would be remiss if it did not include a discussion of outrageous, ingenious, impudent deceits. As you have been told above, successful reproductions often outwit the members of the entrenched art community and tear away their fig leaves to expose their bare naiveté. In France, forgery is such a formidable threat to the connoisseurs that discovered fakes are often confiscated and destroyed by the government even where there is no attempt to deceive and cheat the consumer.

But some collectors respect clever con artists who beat the system, and they are willing to pay big money for successful admitted forgeries.

Elmyr de Hory (1911-1976) was a very talented, prolific copyist who sold hundreds of forgeries to supposedly experienced, knowledgeable curators, museum gurus, and art dealers. The irony is that some of his paintings, for example, copies of Dufys and Toulouse Lautrecs, are considered by some experts to be superior to the original masterpieces. In fact, the recognized artist Kees van Dongan even authenticated one of de Hory's forgeries as his very own original painting!

In the period between 1946 and 1968 de Hory sold more than 1,000 fakes for an estimated $60 million to, among others, Texas "oilionaires," Harvard's Fogg Art Museum, and New York's Museum of Modern Art. A former London book producer bought many of de Hory's works fully aware of their status and has been doing a prosperous business in these bogus originals.

So, if you spot a captivating fake Picasso, van Gogh, Modigliani, or other big name among your possessions, think positively. Well-executed forgeries of the works of such famous masters are in high demand in certain insider quarters. Yours may qualify . . .

Certain artpieces or paintings, not fakes, may fall into a gray area and should be considered for what they are. You may see words on or referring to a painting that you may not understand. The terms "attributed to," "after," "in the manner (style) of," or similar words mean only that the piece was fashioned or painted by an unknown individual who created a work resembling that of the named artist. It could also mean that the artisan worked with or was a student of the famous artist, e.g., a member of the Flemish school or a colleague of Rembrandt.

F. LIMITED EDITIONS

LIMITED TO WHAT?

The concept of collecting "Limited Editions" originated by chance in nineteenth century Denmark. Tradition was that household servants would line up every Christmas to accept gifts of cakes, cookies, and other pastries from members of the family. These tokens would be presented on handmade decorated plates. Once the sweets were eaten, the plates were hung on the wall and eventually became heirlooms.

This custom was formalized by Harald Bing, a director of the pottery factory Bing and Grondahl. In 1895, he commissioned artist F.A. Hallin to handpaint a commemorative Christmas holiday gift plate. Thus was born the legendary blue and white "Behind the Frozen Window," the first collector plate. History was made, and thereafter a Christmas plate was designed and executed each Christmas for Bing and Grondahl by an award winning-artist.

"Little Mermaid," one of the few surviving limited edition 1962 Royal Copenhagen Christmas plates.

Only 400 of the 1895 plate were made, after which Mr. Bing instructed his astonished workers to smash the mold. So this edition was without question limited to those produced from the original mold. When issued, that plate cost two kroner (about 50 cents). It is now worth thousands of dollars, if found.

Technically, the term "limited edition" today means an object produced in a run of a certain specified number. When that number is reached, the original mold or pattern is destroyed, and production ceases forever. However, in current usage, limited can mean various different things:

1) Limited by a pre-determined number. The manufacturer will plan to produce, for example, a total of 5,000 copies. Sometimes each piece is officially assigned a number to indicate its sequence in the production run. When the total number is reached, the original mold is supposed to be destroyed so production is over, never to be resumed.

2) Limited by the specific term during which manufacture goes on, for example, one year. In this case, the number produced is unknown.

3) Limited by a cut-off date, at which time the mold is to be destroyed. How many are made in that time can depend upon the duration of the actual production period, the demand activity, and the manufacturer's production capacity.

4) Limited by the announced number of firing days. The number produced in those days is unknown.

To be realistic, we assume that most editions continue to be produced and marketed as long as orders keep coming in prior to the cut-off date, if one is announced.

Nowadays, activity in limited editions of "manufactured-to-be-collectible" objects has gone berserk. What we have is a burgeoning, widely-promoted industry that floods the market with a plethora of purportedly limited, therefore scarce, appealing articles whose artistic and investment value is not verifiable. The new categories coming on the scene have proliferated wildly and are touted as sure-fire money makers. Because they are advertised as small production runs, the consumer is enticed with the prediction that demand is bound to far exceed supply and resale (secondary) prices will soar.

Every mass-market magazine and publication is loaded with colorful, seductive "Limited Edition" offerings of every imaginable kind of article. It used to be mostly plates, figurines, mugs, dolls, and lithographs. But now it's . . .

Miniature carousel rose clock
American Eagle Bowie knife
Commemorative Elvis Presley signature pen
Egyptian Bast Goddess cat
Star Trek 30-year plate
Radko kaleidoscope
Anders "Treasures of the Heart" miniature plate
Commemorative Ellis Island doll
Various fancy chess sets
and on and on and on . . .

You may also have noticed tempting advertisements by The Washington Mint, LLC, offering "World's First $100 Silver Proof" and by the American Family Coin Co. offering the "United States' First Dollar Coin." Read these ads very carefully, and call the given 800 number to find out about these coins. Some such offerings may be specially minted souvenir, collector coins.

Promoters and distributors liken trading in limited edition collectibles with trading in stocks on Wall Street. This is, of course, an impracticable, ludicrous procedure when we compare sending physical articles back and forth over the miles to transmitting stock via telecommunications.

The only ones making a killing in this "investment" activity are the manufacturers/dealers. The language of their advertised offerings is fuzzy and inexact:

"Forever limited to the exact number reserved (ordered) by the final deadline date."

Annual Lalique crystal plate, Limited Edition No. 7.

"Exclusive limited edition."
"A limited fine art sculpture, individually hand numbered."
"Only 3,500 people in the world will ever own this plate."
"Will be closed forever after just 45 firing days."

Such ads are vague and confusing. Most manufacturers announce that they will fire for only a specified number of days—45, 95, or 150, for example. Nowhere and in no way do the factories reveal their firing capacity, their rate of production, or their total output. The firing may be done on consecutive days; or it may be done every other day, one day a week, or according to whatever schedule the plant decides to follow. Conclusion: If the limitation is thus undefinable, the total output can fluctuate with the whim or commercial self-interest of the manufacturer.

Following is a tongue-in-cheek advertisement run by the *New York Times* on November 17, 1972, expressing amusement at the course of this boom and the lengths to which it has proliferated. It is worth a good chuckle since it is applicable today, twenty-seven years later.

"LIMITED EDITIONS"

"This season seems to be replete with offers of so-called collector's items issued in 'Limited Editions,' often represented as Great Art, but too often of questionable artistic merit. Some of them are huckstered with sophisticated 20th Century versions of the snake-oil technique of the 19th Century calculated to appeal to the greed of the customer with implied promises of increased future value, as well as with attempts to scare the customer into a quick purchase or else this "priceless golden opportunity" will be gone forever.

"So, to top all Limited Editions once and for all, we offer the celebrated 128 carat Tiffany Diamond, the largest and finest Canary Diamond in the world, in a Limited Edition of 'one' for the sum of $5,000,000. What's more, in our judgment, past history and everything else considered, it will easily be worth $10,000,000 one hundred years from now.

"Mail orders will not be accepted if postmarked after November 17, 1972. First-come, first served, of course."

Tiffany & Co.
New York

If, all things considered, you have invested in or acquired or need to estimate monetary value to cash in on your limited editions, bear in mind:

The best, most valued materials of limited editions are silver, porcelain, and crystal.

It helps to find out the number actually produced of a specific edition. More than 20,000 is a glut on the market.

If the name of the designer/artist is Hummel, Boehm, Hibel, or another of that caliber, the article is more valuable.

The criteria for the merit of the article are genuine artistic and aesthetic quality, technical perfection, precious material, and intrinsic virtue.

The original box, documents, and authenticating evidence are very important when selling. "Mint in Box" greatly enhances the price.

Whether the market is on a Bull or Bear trend, the stock exchange is best reserved for trading in securities and shares of stock, not dishes.

What is all this fretting and fussing about the "genuine/original article" leading up to? Why, the money you can get for it, of course. You are going to have to find out what your possessions are worth on the market.

In the next chapter, you will learn many ways to assess the value of a variety of articles—to discover the tricks of the trade, the appraising trade, that is. Thus, you will join the "inner circle!"

CHAPTER FOUR

HOW TO EVALUATE WHAT YOU HAVE

"I often wonder what the vintners buy
One-half so precious as the stuff they sell"
— "The Rubiyat of Omar Khayyam"
by Edward Fitzgerald

What is it worth? This is one of the most important, and perplexing, questions you face when planning to dispose of your accumulated possessions. You may be grossly underestimating or simply do not know the value of what you have. After all, those familiar objects have been around forever, and, to your unpracticed eye, they look like and are being treated like unimportant trinkets.

But take another look at that vintage pewter cup that you have been using as a catch-all for buttons, coins, paper clips, and mateless earrings; the old, handmade baby's quilt you keep at the back door for wiping shoes; the charming folk-art whirligig that you casually offer to a neighbor's child to play with; and the sad looking Victorian nightstand that you plan to donate to the Salvation Army.

These are misguided impulses. We all make such mistakes. If you do not take the time to do your homework, you will never know the real monetary value of your surplus or unwanted items, and you risk giving away something important and precious. All kinds of resources are readily available to research mystery objects, mostly cost-free.

In Chapter Three you have learned how to identify, authenticate, and label all your possessions. Now your miscellaneous articles should be sorted and grouped in similar categories. This will simplify the job of looking up their value.

Pewter was used in olden times for dinnerware and utensils in place of costly china or silver. The dull finish on this old pewter cup indicates a lot of lead in the lead, copper, and tin composition.

There are many reasons for determining an article's worth on the current market:
• To sell it.
• To provide an accurate assessment for insurance purposes.
•To evaluate for a tax-deductible charitable donation.
• To set a specified amount in your will as protection against its sale for an unrealistic or arbitrary figure during probate.
• And, of course, to satisfy your curiosity.

As you undertake the appraisal of your assorted possessions, you should understand the difference between replacement cost and fair market value because these figures have a direct effect upon the evaluation of your articles.

Replacement cost, the amount used for insurance claims, is what a buyer would have to pay in a retail store or other commercial outlet to replace what he lost through theft, fire, breakage, etc. In the vernacular, it is the amount that would have to be paid for an item comparable in quality to the one insured, considering all markets foreign and domestic. Where you will find that specific comparable item is up to you, but a retail establishment is a source acceptable to your insurer.

Fair market value is established by a different criterion. It is the price at which the item would change hands—again in legalese—between any willing buyer and willing seller, neither party being under any compulsion to buy or sell and both parties having reasonable knowledge of the relevant facts about the object. This fair market value figure is the one that is used for tax-deductible charitable donations and computing federal estate taxes.

By way of explanation, let us hypothesize that an Oriental rug (or painting, or article of vintage furniture, or rare antique) may sell in an antique store for $10,000 yet could bring only $3,000 in an estate sale. For insurance purposes, it should be valued at $10,000, the amount that would have to be paid in a store that offers the article to the general buying public, to replace it. For estate tax purposes it would, however, be valued at $3,000, the fair market value arrived at as the result of negotiations between individual buyer and seller, such as might take place privately at an estate sale, garage sale, etc.

Conversely, if an item is purchased for $3,000 and it later brings $10,000 at auction, the newer figure of $10,000 becomes the fair market value (the current replacement cost) for insurance purposes.

Property to be donated to a charity must be appraised by a qualified, credentialed expert; the Internal Revenue Service has the services of an Art Advisory Panel that uses specific, rigid guidelines to review submitted appraisals of donated artwork. You need to know this in case you intend to avail yourself of a tax advantage by donating something to a charity or other qualified recipients (complete details about this procedure are provided in Chapter Five).

A. PRICE DETERMINANTS

WHAT FACTORS INFLUENCE A PRICE?

An article's merit or monetary worth is rated according to its rarity, artistry, antiquity, and condition. These qualities will

Three views of an antique Capodimonte lidded box with polychrome allegorical figures. "Ardalt Capodimonte 4669 Italy" is marked on the bottom.

impact the item's market price at a certain time, in a certain geographic location, or during certain economic conditions.

Be aware of a variety of factors that affect prices and activate trends and fluctuations.

AGE AND AUTHENTICITY

Is a modern piece likely to be undervalued and under-appreciated because it is not an "antique"? (see p. 52 for a definition of antique). Answer: YES, often.

Is age more important than signature or rarity? Answer: It all depends. For example, many inexperienced collectors of Shaker furniture or handicrafts seem to prefer the later, more plentiful production pieces because they are signed and therefore seemingly a guarantee of authenticity. Yet, ironically, the earlier, much finer Shaker articles were deliberately not signed.

In the case of art glass, be skeptical when examining a piece that is "signed." Manufacturers have been known to sign their fake products with the name of a famous, reputable company to give them legitimacy. When an expert compares the fake piece with the genuine, he relies heavily upon the ABSENCE of a signature to verify the original.

SCARCITY

A damaged article of fine quality and artistry made by a skilled, superior artisan who produced only a few pieces is much more desirable and expensive than a mint specimen made by a prolific, mediocre craftsman.

Rare decoys made by painstaking, talented carvers command enormous prices. For example, a meticulously designed and executed wooden Canada goose with a hollow body created by Harry V. Shourds in Tuckerton, New Jersey, is valued at upwards of $60,000; a rare redhead drake made by skilled artisan Charles Perdew of Illinois was sold for $43,500; and an old squaw drake made by Joseph W. Lincoln ca. 1900 was valued at $26,000.

LOCATION

As said above, experts usually evaluate an item according to a specific market trend at a specific time or season in a specific geographical location. An item of little or no interest at an auction in mid-Manhattan might be in great demand in the Midwestern states or even right across town on the West Side.

Authentic architectural antiques are avidly sought and are valued very high by specialized collectors. Buildings are not being razed with the same indifference and abandon as in years ago, and all kinds of architectural and decorating artifacts are highly prized. They are usually snatched up by dealers before the first blow demolishing the building is struck.

The location of these spoils has a great bearing on their market price. For example, an iron gate or ornate molding trim from a New Orleans historic mansion may be acquired on the site for a "steal." Yet, this same item may bring a price many times higher when sold to a wealthy, determined buyer thousands of miles away in New York or Seattle.

Garden statuary and wrought iron grillwork adorned old mansions in New Orleans and Savannah. Such archaeological spoils were rescued from historical landmarks being demolished in the name of progress.

CONDITION

Flaked paint, dents, chips, or missing parts may totally devaluate a collectible. Repairs may or may not enhance the

Turbo Firebird Bandit, the ERTL Co., Dyersville, Iowa.

market price. An expert repair to an old, sturdy, vintage country rocking chair may legitimately increase the value. However, a new coat of paint on an old, rare metal toy car or figure will drastically lower the price; the item would be worth much more with

A very old, fully armored and equipped cast-iron diver, numbered 65.

its old, peeling paint.

Attempting to repair cracks or imperfections in old books, limited edition artpieces, or other rarities greatly reduces their value. Do not try to refinish antique furniture. Very minute scratches can be covered inconspicuously with a commercial stain polish and scratch remover.

MARKET MANIPULATION

A dealer in the doldrums hit on an idea for moving and cashing in on a stagnant, drab line of pottery manufactured in the early 1900s. He quietly amassed enough of these wares to corner the market. Then he built up a prestige base for his jugs and vases by designing and printing a fancy catalog, preparing a history of the artisans/makers, and then reluctantly agreeing to lend his beloved collection to gullible curators of small museums hungry for quick, ready-to-show exhibits. There were plenty of willing curators.

The scenario was in place, and the production debuted on the road. With a portfolio of museum citations and flattering press reviews along with an "official" documented history, the sharp dealer marketed his wares. Any auctioneer is captivated by "museum quality" pieces to put on the block. Publicity was in full swing and prices soared.

This same successful strategy is practiced with different items and techniques. Modus operandi: Corner the market, create a powerful magnet of popular demand, and sell quickly into that demand. Articles so promoted and publicized have included cookie jars, lace artifacts, Swatch watches, and ceramic products produced by the late Russel Wright, whose mundane dishes and furniture skyrocketed in value after gaining the credentials of being exhibited in a museum.

ERRATIC GUIDELINES

An article's value is often based upon an estimate by a "professional" of its worth to a potential buyer. The least stable figures are those provided in special indexes compiled by individual commercial enterprises. Prices obtained from such sources should be studied and analyzed carefully.

Computerized indexes are accepted at face value without question by most users. The listed figures should be examined for their source and for the special information they provide; they are often reports of certain types of sales by specialized outlets. For example, prestigious auction houses periodically publish prices fetched for various antiques and collectibles. But these prices are those paid at the auctions of a particular house, too rarefied and unstandardized a segment to reflect the general market.

Furthermore, the categories sometimes are too broad to be meaningful as specific indicators. For instance, of what use is the information that "Furniture" rose in value but "English Pine" fell? This is a distinction that the print-out of the sold-at prices does not explain.

A well-known postage stamp index a few years ago drastically revised and downgraded the values it had formerly listed for many collectible stamps. It arbitrarily decided to switch from using dealers' prices to independently monitoring and publishing its own figures. Where, then, went the erstwhile stable standard whereby to determine actual market values?

Another source that turned out to be vague and non-specific is an index that had been devised by an important investment firm. Its catalog of prices comprised various classifications of assets that included stamps and coins. The coin segment reflected a selected hypothetical collection, NOT actual sales of specific coins. Not only that, it failed to factor in important expenses such as costs of insurance, storage, and trading. For stamps, this same firm relied upon the undependable unstable guide referred to above.

Another unrealistic influence upon prices is the so-called "halo" effect of artificial, manufactured values. This is an artifice that automatically inflates and enhances items exhibited in museums and galleries; featured in books and brochures; and publicized in newspapers, periodicals, and art magazines.

In short, published price listings cannot be depended upon like stock market quotations, which are actual documented trading prices. Be wise and do as successful insiders do—investigate and verify the source of the data. And be aware that many guides are privately printed by dealers, high-volume collectors, and traders who find it to their advantage to purposely create puffed up fictitious prices for their own commercial benefit.

PRICE-INCREASING FEATURES

Here is a list of special attributes that have demonstrated they add to the value of items being offered for sale. See which, if any, your saleables have:
• Mint condition.

• Original box. Mint in box (MIB) commands a premium; Mint in original, unopened box (MOB) a higher premium.

• Reliable provenance (see pp. 70-71).

• Directions and instructions that came with the item.

• Event-related items, such as souvenirs of World Fairs or Expositions, coronations, political campaigns, etc.

• Popular, high-demand manufacturers/designers, e.g., Hummel, Avon, Lalique, Baccarat, R.S. Prussia, Faberge, etc.

• A matched pair brings much more than the same item(s) sold singly; a full set is worth more than the sum of its parts.

• Occupation or trade-related objects like medical, cobbler, or blacksmith instruments and tools.

• Documents or objects related to local or national history.

• Objects related to movements: civil rights, women's rights, etc.

Will Rogers Baccarat sulphide paperweight, 1970. (Courtesy Twana Barnett, Vero Beach, Florida.)

• The "naughty" factor, a term introduced by a prestigious New York City auctioneer. He said, the more erotic the piece, the higher the price, e.g., items relating to alcohol, tobacco, gambling, sex, etc.

This pair of rare Roseville candlesticks exemplifies the potter's soft time-worn quality, muted colors, and matte finish.

B. THE BOTTOM LINE

WHAT PRICE ENDS UP ON THE TAG?

There are many ways to arrive at the dollar number you will place on the price tag of the article you want to sell. The asking price should represent fair market value because you are offering your merchandise on the open market.

In deciding what price you will put on the tag, you have two options:

1) Do your own research and decide on a reasonable figure. You have access to the same information sources that practicing appraisers use. These are described throughout this chapter. So, if you have the time, energy, and motivation, you can do a pretty good job yourself unless you are dealing with unfamiliar, special rarities like Georgian silver, Oriental rugs, antique furniture, or other articles beyond your capabilities.

2) Use professional services and resources: appraisers, results of auctions, price lists and guides, and computer data. These are discussed in detail in the following pages.

I. PROFESSIONAL APPRAISAL
HIRE AN EXPERT

Finding a competent, thoroughly informed, reputable appraiser is a job. There are many who advertise, but it is up to you to verify their qualifications and credentials. There is no state or national certification, registration, or licensing procedure for appraisers (as for doctors, lawyers, CPAs, etc.), so anyone can call himself an appraiser.

If you should ask someone you are considering, "Are you a certified appraiser?" you may get a "yes" answer, but the meaning of that "yes" can be confusing. Since there is no agency to do the certifying, no one can be officially certified; hence the "yes" answer means something else, to-wit: Some appraisal forms may read, "I hereby certify that the following appraisal is . . . " What this means is simply that the appraiser is the certifier of certain facts; it does not mean that he is himself certified. There is a difference.

Bear in mind a very important thing when seeking appraisals. Use discretion if you turn your entire household or collection to be evaluated by one know-it-all expert or service. There is no such animal. There are specialists in this business just as in the medical and legal worlds. No single person or organization can be fully informed about the millions of objects that have been made, studied, and sold throughout history. For certain items, you may need to consult an appraiser with special expertise.

An appraisal, whether of artwork, antiques, jewelry, real estate, or miscellaneous collectibles, is an opinion, an art. It is NOT a science that uses an established formula to reach a result or a conclusion. To be realistic, there can never be a set, immutable, universally agreed upon and relied upon price for any one item.

The appraising profession itself is undefined, unregulated, and unstandardized. It is highly subjective and beset with problems of expertise and ethics. There are as many appraisers and wannabe appraisers as there are categories of articles being bought, collected, and offered for sale. The experts and professionals often spend countless hours and consult many reference sources before they venture an estimate of the value of the items under study. In no way can a single "authority" appraise an estate or a collection comprising many different categories on the basis of his own narrow expertise or experience.

So, to get professional help, find at least two authorities competent in the specific category of articles you are concerned with. Be sure to check out the credentials of the firm you are considering.

Some appraisers claim to offer "all-purpose expertise," calling themselves "generalists." This is a doubtful recommendation because it has no real meaning and does not focus on a specific field of artwork or collectibles. Some, on the other hand, have become very knowledgeable in certain categories—furniture, fine arts, jewelry, Oriental rugs, musical instruments, art glass, and other particular types of articles. Find out exactly what experience and expertise the firm has with items like yours.

Conflict of interest: Appraisers often wear different hats in addition to appraiser, namely, dealer in antiques, auctioneer, interior decorator, art consultant, used-furniture salesman, pawn shop owner, and various others.

The occasional, maybe innocent, conflict of interest that may occur is understandable. When does a dealer stop dealing and become an objective appraiser? Can he or she remain uninfluenced by the possibility that he may someday be able to return to your home and buy the item appraised? However, you may get an argument that, because they are active in the marketplace and know what a piece should sell for, dealers are better qualified to know the value of the item than an appraiser who is not a dealer.

The American Society of Appraisers (see pp. 100-101 for a full discussion of organizations) recognizes that some dealers are qualified appraisers and has this to say on the subject:

" . . . it is unethical and unprofessional for an appraiser to accept an assignment to appraise a property *in which he has an interest or a contemplated future interest.* However, if a prospective client, after full disclosure by the appraiser of his present or contemplated future interest in the subject property, still desires to have that appraiser do the work, the latter may properly accept the engagement, provided he disclosed the nature and extent of his interest *in his appraisal report.*" (italics added).

Until the growing demand for appraisers who confine their activities to appraising can be met, the public will be forced to use appraisers who are also dealers. However, you may ask for a signed statement of disinterest in the property if the appraiser does not already include such a clause in his final appraisal report.

Ivory Tower (Museum) Appraisals: Most museums decree that their staff members cannot quote or suggest values in their official capacities. Even museums that feature "heirloom" or "discovery" days, when the public may bring in articles to be identified, authenticated, and dated, do NOT appraise or evaluate these items.

Some museum personnel do "moonlight" by performing appraisals (in their own names as independent contractors) on their days off. On the plus side, museum personnel do have access to archives, research material, specialists, and esoteric information unavailable to many appraisers. On the negative side: Though they can identify and date a piece quickly and accurately, they may not know its current market value because keeping up with the rapidly changing market-place is a full time job that is not within the capability of the museum personnel.

Choosing the Right Appraiser: Just as one selects an employee or retains an attorney, the place to start is with an interview. Here are some specific questions to ask:

1) How long have you been an appraiser?

2) What is your area of specialization or expertise?

3) For whom have you done appraisals and what are your references (individual households, businesses, banks, insurance companies, museums, etc. — check them out).

4) Are you a member of a professional appraisal organization? Which? (see pp. 100-101 for some organizations).

5) How do you arrive at your values? (The candidate should have a comprehensive reference library; would attend and gain information from auctions; attend seminars and conferences on antiques and collectibles; and have extensive, regularly updated price guides and indexes.).

Do not engage a "flexible" appraiser who hedges and waivers in an effort to guess at the figure he thinks you want. Look for a forthright, trustworthy person. There are plenty of dependable professionals out there. Feel free to comparison shop and look for more than one opinion.

Your Inventory: Before setting an appointment date and following through with the actual appraisal, you can facilitate the whole procedure and save considerable money that you would be paying for appraising time if you:

• Organize your thoughts and your assorted property.

• Separate your articles into two groups: (1) items that you can identify and document and (2) items that you cannot find information about.

• Gather together earlier appraisals, bills of sale, and receipts and attach them to or place them upon the item to which they belong.

• Arrange crystal, silver, china, etc., in groups of the same pattern.

• Separate sterling from plated, or inferior silver.

Doing all of the above in advance is bound to reduce your appraising bill, especially if you are paying on an hourly or daily basis.

Appraisers' Charges: Agree upon and establish fees in advance. First be aware of practices that you should not agree to:

1) Refuse percentage fees. There are some appraisers who charge a percentage of the value of the item they appraise. This is an unethical practice, an invitation to fraud, i.e., gross overvaluation of the article in order to get a correspondingly inflated commission. Just think: What if that bronze you "stole" at a flea market for $175 turns out to be a genuine Barye worth $30,000. You could be charged a fee of 3 percent, or $900!

Another case in point: An appraiser who works on a percentage basis might say, for example, "Your antique reverse painting lamp is worth at least $9,000 and my commission is 3 percent, or $270. Now consider this—We are looking at the same lamp. He wants to buy it and suddenly it's a pathetic

The high appraisal of this antique crystal decanter is attributable to its artistic design, skilled craftsmanship, and lavish gold trim.

This signed Lalique perfume bottle has a stopper in the form of a pair of doves.

Tiffany reproduction worth $300 tops, and he'll do you a big favor and take it off your hands right now for $250 and save you the trouble of trying to sell it!

2) Refuse contingent fees. This is when an appraiser tells you he will appraise "high" an item that you want to sell or take a tax donation on, in return for a share of the tax benefit; or conversely, he will appraise an item "low" for estate purposes for a cut of the taxes saved. These contingent arrangements are so blatantly immoral that the American Society of Appraisers in its Code of Ethics calls them unprofessional, unethical, and self serving.

For a house visit, the majority of good appraisers charge on an hourly or daily basis, ranging from $35 to $150 an hour or $350 to $1,500 per day. You may also be charged for research time. If your job does not seem large or difficult enough to warrant a formal written contract, ask the appraiser to spell out the exact working terms for this situation before he makes the house visit.

The appraiser may be considerate enough to work with you if you are uncertain about the identity or value of one or more of your items, which may turn out to be of negligible value or importance. When you set the appointment, ask the appraiser

This antique Japanese fancy cup had been purposely crackled (crazed) in the process of manufacture to achieve a unique decorative effect.

Royal Doulton Dickensware plate, 10" diameter, depicting a bootblack at a London station, signed "Sam Weller."

if he would settle for a token fee if he can tell right away that your precious "heirloom" vase is a Woolworth ca. 1976 bauble.

Feel free to ask the appraiser for an estimate of what your bill may be. For large jobs, the appraiser may make a preliminary visit to your home and, for a nominal fee, give you a rough idea of the total cost.

Hand-painted, polychrome, gold decorated Nippon candy dish with handle.

Tell the appraiser what to expect. For example: "I have a seven-room house, approximately 2,500 square feet, and various antiques, heirlooms, and collectibles that need appraising for estate division (or insurance purposes, or whatever). There will also be about thirty pieces of furniture and many accessories, such as sets of silver flatware, hollowware, three sets of china, two sets of crystal, a box of antique linens, and twenty to thirty decorative articles including collectible limited editions, fine art, decanters, and other artifacts.

This is enough information to suggest that the better part of a day will be needed for the appraisal. Based upon, for example, $70 an hour, the appraiser calculates the bill might be $500 to $600, and you can then make up your mind.

What You Get for Your Money: For your $500 or $600, you should receive two copies of a professionally prepared document containing the appraiser's best judgment of the age, features, physical condition, and, if possible, the national origin of each piece. When the maker is known—company, craftsman, or artist—that will be included. Number or sets will be specified. And finally, each item or set will be assigned a value appropriate to the purpose of the appraisal—insurance, private sale, estate taxes, whatever the case may be. The date and the purpose of the appraisal and the appraiser's signature must always be shown.

A scribbled, handwritten appraisal with incorrect spelling, insufficient details, and inaccurate figures and information is not acceptable. For example, "8 blue velvet armless dining room chairs, $2,000" means nothing. There is no age, description, manufacturer, or condition. Getting a sloppy or inadequate appraisal is like patching a leaking fuel tank with glue and Scotch tape. Useless.

What You Cannot Expect to Get for Your Money: For your $500 or $600 you will not have every single obscure article in your house researched, authenticated, and evaluated. If you have an heirloom you consider rare, valuable, or unusual, call it to the attention of the appraiser and ask if he can identify and evaluate it. A good appraiser knows what is outside his area of expertise and can either accept and complete the job to the best of his ability or make a helpful referral to a specialist.

Appraisal Associations: Because the demand for appraisers is steadily increasing, more and more inexperienced, unqualified appraisers as well as questionable organizations have sprung up overnight. All such bodies have to do is give themselves an impressive name and manufactured credentials and they're in business.

A wannabe appraiser gains instant respectability by joining an organization. To become a member, all he does is fill out an entry form and send it to "headquarters" with the required fee, which can range from $10 to $1,000 or more. Some of these organizations can be compared with mail-order colleges where for a specified amount you receive a diploma to hang on your wall.

However, there are several fine, authentic appraisal organizations that do valuable, necessary work. You may want to check out some of the specialized, locally situated societies that are available to help you. Following are the three most important appraisal organizations that have been recognized and respected nationwide. Feel free to ask them for their membership rosters or the name of a member in your area.

1) The Appraisers Association of America, a national organization headquartered in New York City, was founded in 1949 to provide standards for ethical conduct of appraisers and to promote the advancement of skill and honor among its members. It defines the fiduciary roles and responsibilities of an appraiser as clearly as those of a lawyer or a doctor. It is a good source of qualified appraisers throughout the country, explaining their exact fields of specialization:

Appraisers Association of America (AAA)
386 Park Ave. S.
New York, NY 10016

2) Another highly regarded appraisers association is the American Society of Appraisers, which was founded in 1952. This is a multidisciplinary service that embraces every facet of the appraising business, both commercial (real estate, machinery, etc.) and art/antique/personal property. Its standards demand that members be qualified, objective, and unbiased. They must have at least five years of evaluation experience and must have passed written and oral examinations on ethics, appraisal principles and guidelines, and their specialized areas:

American Society of Appraisers (ASA)
P.O. Box 17265
Washington, DC 20041

3) The International Society of Appraisers deals with personal property such as the contents of residences, fine arts, antiques, jewelry, etc. It prescreens appraisal specialists:

International Society of Appraisers
16040 Christensen Rd., Suite 320
Seattle, WA 98188

II. AUCTION RESULTS
WHAT DID IT "FETCH"?

One of the most reliable and accurate sources of the actual "sold-at" price of an item is the recorded results of national and international auctions. Although individual auction houses document records of the results of sales, most do not publish and release this information to the general public on a periodic, regular basis. The best source of such figures is the New York Public Library.

The Library breaks down the auction results in a *User's Guide Index,* which lists a full complement of art, antique, furniture, jewelry, photography, and many other categories.

Anyone may check the *Index* to find the item classification and the time, place, and auction house conducting the sale. The *Index* provides compilations of prices realized, descriptions of the sold articles, and other helpful information.

To obtain a copy of the *User's Guide Index* and other guidelines to help in your research, write to:

The New York Public Library
Art and Architecture Division
Fifth Avenue and 42nd St.
New York, NY 10018

In reviewing auction figures, bear in mind the often quirky, unexpected factors that may have gone into play to result in the "sold-at" price:

• Auction fever or bidding mania, meaning being uncontrollably caught up in the hectic game.

• An emotional, nostalgic attachment to the article

• A duel between adamant adversaries.

• The item came from a publicized estate; a show business, political, or sports personality; or royalty.

So, obviously, all sorts of circumstances and influences affect the final price. Yet this auction result goes on record as the statistic most often quoted as an authentic reflection of market demand. Take these forces into account and use your best judgment in analyzing and using the auction information.

Here's something to think about: The big auction houses publish a pre-sale catalog of their important sales providing estimates of what they think each item might bring. A comparison of these figures with the final realized prices is often a surprise.

III. PRICE LISTS, GUIDES, AND OTHER SOURCES
LOOK UP THE NUMBERS AND USE THEM WISELY

Price guides serve as an indispensable tool for collectors, traders, and finally, sellers. The collecting passion, which has generated a $20 billion-plus manufacturing industry, is rampant in antique malls, flea markets, and collector meets and conventions. This body of accumulators needs to look up the value of the articles they want to buy, or at the other end of the process, to sell. To meet this demand, so-called price guides and price lists are being churned out by the score. These compilations are for sale not only in book stores and over the Internet, but in the most popular and profitable stalls at flea markets and malls.

Many years ago, Ralph and Terry Kovel pioneered in the production and dissemination of collectibles books covering every conceivable category. Their annually upgraded price guides are a staple among researchers.

The Antique Trader's *Antiques and Collectibles Price Guide* takes the reader above and beyond the scope of just a list of prices. It is a comprehensive and descriptive reference work providing the most current, accurate information culled from experts in the field. It furnishes historical background and data about many categories; covers classic as well as modern collectibles; and spells out determinants of market value.

Recently, leading mass-market publishers have jumped on the bandwagon: Ballantine Books produces the *House of Collectibles* price guide; Avon Books, *The Confident Collector;* and Lyles, the *Official Antiques Review.* To top it all, Christie's and Sotheby Parke Bernet are joining the fun with their own series of collectibles guides.

The overriding question has to be: What exactly are the figures listed in these guides? Do they help us in our purchasing decisions and, especially, in putting a price tag on our articles we want to sell?

Answer: What these guides do is give us an idea of what an object may be worth and what its asking price is. They do not tell us what someone is ready, willing, and able to pay for it with cash (or check) in hand. The thing to always bear in mind is that a price guide is just that—a guide—not an ironclad standard of monetary worth in the marketplace. It cannot tell you how much you will get for an article like the one described in the book. Unlike daily final stock quotations, a guide does not give the dollar sum for which the item was last sold on a given day, thus indicating how much it might, barring unusual events, open for in the stock market the next morning.

Some of the information used by the compilers comes from auction results, but most guides rely on surveys of dealers at antique fairs, flea markets, and ads in trade magazines. These are not necessarily final prices paid, for example, for a Jim Beam bottle, a Mickey Mouse Emerson radio, a Shaker seed box, or a painted antique tole serving tray. The figures are usually the asking prices, which naturally fluctuate with the negotiating process and other current conditions.

With all this in mind, professionals and experienced researchers, for lack of better sources, resort to price guides for

Occupational mugs are valued if they contain the name of the owner, the symbol or picture of his trade, and especially his photograph. Professional motifs are hard to find owing to the former reluctance (prohibition) of doctors, lawyers, and other rarefied species to advertise.

their information but they use the data for what it is worth and with full knowledge of its limitations.

In practice, a price list or guide can be compared with the well-known "Blue Book," which is used for estimating current market values for used cars.

There are two types of price guides: general and specific.

General guides contain many thousands of items, as many as can be conveniently presented in one volume. Most general guides are compiled and printed by computer; the writers could not possibly have seen untold thousands of articles with their own eyes.

As for specific guides, hundreds have been printed and new ones come on the scene as fresh novelty items are produced, marketed, and collected. Each such compilation focuses on one currently popular collectible and is usually printed in a relatively small production run. The data dealing with certain well-established, classical categories such as Roseville pottery, occupational shaving mugs, Carnival glass, napkin rings, vintage bottles, and pattern glass are pretty stable, and guides dealing with such articles can look forward to a long life span. Others, which are kitsch, campy, or "passing fancy" items, can lose their original appeal and fade away after an initial splash.

Compilers of general guides list their contents by category, sub-category, and sometimes particular features, for example:

CATEGORY	SUB-CATEGORY
FIGURINES	Hummel, Stangl, Royal Doulton
ART GLASS	Murano, Steuben, Labino, Tiffany
FOLK ART	Weather vanes, whirligigs, decoys

To find the methodology of the guide you are using, look at the introductory preface or road map provided by the compiler. Among other things, you will be told that the prices shown are for the most part neither top level nor bargain basement figures but middle of the range as traded in the general market. No price shown is an estimate; it is the actual asking price, negotiable downward when dealing with a bona fide prospective buyer.

Mass-market listings as reported in price guides and indexes vary and fluctuate with date and season, market trends, geographic location, and authenticity/provenance of the particular article. The principal purpose of the guide is to

Rare vintage bowl with gold highlights, hallmarked "Stangl Pottery," Trenton, New Jersey.

indicate and compare the relative worth of specific items based upon the following criteria:
- Fame and credentials of the artisan or manufacturer.
- Craftsmanship, creativity, and artistry.
- Color quality.
- Origin (period, culture, ethnic derivation).
- Age.
- Condition.

For example, if the listing shows that a tureen that seems to be identical to another carries a price double that of the first, you may (or may not) be told that the higher priced one has superior, innovative glazework or color intensity.

OR a Carnival glass pitcher of the Grape Arbor pattern, normally priced at a few hundred dollars, was listed at a record $14,000 because its color was an unusual, seldom seen shade of deep blue-green.

OR an entry describing a mahogany Empire sofa with scrolled arms listed the price at $550; a similarly described sofa was $2,200 because it pointed out far superior carving and near-mint condition.

AND still another example: A Murano glass bowl that was usually produced in four popular colors was priced at $50.

The guide did not mention that a very small quantity of this same bowl was also made in a fifth color, a rare shade of amber, and priced at $600.

The message is that it will be to your advantage to learn all you can about the methodology used in the reporting of prices. Carefully read the explanatory material at the beginning of the guide you are referring to. It will tell you exactly what information is provided, how it was obtained, and what use it will be to you, the would-be seller.

Following are just a few of the numerous available price guides and other selling aids that will help in your pricing and marketing research.

General Guides (most are updated annually):
- *The Antique Trader Antiques and Collectibles Price Guide,* Antique Trader Books, edited by Kyle Husfloen.
- *Collectors Information Bureau: Collectibles Market Guide and Price Index,* distributed by Wallace Homestead.
- *Schroeder's Antiques Price Guide,* Collector Books, Schroeder Publishing Co.
- *Warman's Antiques and Collectibles Price Guide,* edited by Harry L. Rinker.

Specific Guides: Among the countless specific guides on the market are those dealing with arrowheads, razor blades, white ironstone, crackerjack prizes, and Texaco signs. There are at least a dozen guides each on Teddy Bears, stamps, coins, and Barbie dolls. Here are just a few of the current titles published by Antique Trader Books:

- *The Postcard Price Guide,* by J. L. Washburn.
- *Petretti's Coca-Cola Collectibles Price Guide,* by Allan Petretti.
- *Die Cast Price Guide,* by Douglas R. Kelly.
- *Black Americana Price Guide,* edited by Kyle Husfloen.

Before wrapping up "Price Guides," here is some information to help you understand how to look up your particular article. As explained in its Preface, *Kovels Antiques and Collectibles Guide* presents its price data as follows:
GENERAL CATEGORY: Furniture
SPECIFIC OBJECT: Mirror
DESCRIPTION . . . . . . Size, material, style, age, etc.

Kovels exercises certain flexibility in its discretion and for practical purposes. For example, it decided to list under the general category TOOLS special equipment such as adze, change sorter, bee smoker, and other items unfamiliar to the inexperienced collector. It also takes the liberty of making certain editorial decisions, calling a bowl simply "bowl" and not a dish unless it is a pickle dish and using the word "button" rather than pinback.

Thus, you see that making good use of price guides requires a familiarity with how the book organizes, classifies, and presents its categories. It would be time well spent to review the system as explained in the front of the book you are using.

Other Resources: In addition to published price guides, certain popular TV programs provide excellent information about the value of various antiques and collectibles. *Antiques Road Show* airing on PBS, for example, explains and appraises all kinds of classical as well as recent collectibles.

The following books written by Dr. H. A. Hyman about how to offer and sell your various and sundry articles will also be of help to you. They are published by Treasure Hunt Publications, Claremont, California.

- *Cash for Your Undiscovered Treasures*
- *The Where to Sell Anything and Everything Book*
- *Where to Sell Anything and Everything by Mail*
- *I'll Buy That*

IV. COMPUTER SEARCH
EXPLORE THE WEB

A very valuable resource for evaluating and marketing your accumulated possessions is the electronic equipment right at your elbow. Computer literate practitioners can with a click of the keys obtain a wealth of information about market prices and other features of specific artifacts and objects that you have acquired over the years and want to sell. You can also locate and communicate with buyers, traders, and professionals who deal with a full range of antiques, heirlooms, and collectibles.

Use the Internet to show you the way: The Internet is a swiftly expanding universe—a huge quantum leap in global communication. It is an enormous network of networks connecting you and your computer with computers all over the world and with the people sitting on antique chairs in front of incongruous high-tech computer cabinets.

In this electronic marketplace you can meet and exchange information with thousands of people who have the same interests, concerns, and needs that you have: collecting, buying, appraising, and selling antiques, artifacts, and household effects.

To plug into the Internet, you must connect your computer to others linked within the so-called Information Superhighway. Once connected, you are on track and can "talk" to other participating computers, whether next door or on the other side of the world.

Your available on-line services, which you select and to which you can subscribe, include nationally recognized companies such as America Online (AOL), Microsoft, and Prodigy. They provide not only Internet access, but various other private content materials. Or you may opt to use a local service for direct Internet access; typically, it may lack the frills of the major providers, but it can save you several dollars each month in connection fees. Check your local yellow pages under the heading "Internet Services."

Consider these computer-derived benefits:

Obtain information—Peruse thousands of websites operated by others interested in collectibles and personal possessions. Look at the prices and other data they provide.

Traverse the Web—Click on the "links" found in these websites to find and explore other websites. Your journey will undoubtedly carry you on a learning experience.

Bookmark interesting sites—Using your web browser software, mark sites you want to explore more fully later (want to share with your cyber buddies).

Build and download databases—As you surf, you will find E-mail and snail-mail addresses of people with whom you may want to stay in touch. Build your own databases. Some sites you visit may even have mailing lists that you can copy and convert for your own purposes. Use them.

Anti-spam advisory: Unsolicited and often widespread E-mail is known as "spam." It targets thousands of recipients at once. It is considered gauche to engage in this activity. To keep your E-mail from being perceived as "spam," ask yourself, "Would I be happy to receive this E-mail or would I be annoyed by it?" Keep E-mail short, relevant, and to the point.

Use chat rooms—These are (1) presented under the auspices of your Internet Service provider (AOL, Prodigy, etc.) and (2) organized by a website somewhere (e.g., come here every Tuesday night at 9 p.m. central time and we'll "talk"). People "sign on" and have interactive communication with others who are online currently.

So these are ways you can pick the brains of participating experts by selecting the newsgroup involved in, for example, Antiques and Collectibles; posting your specific query (sales and marketing avenues, for example); and receive the input of the appropriate source.

Take advantage of a search engine, which is an Internet-based service that enables you to "search" websites on the WWW by using keywords, codes, or phrases describing your specific interest, e.g., Artifacts, Collectibles, Folk Art, Pez Dispensers, Marbles, Tiffany Glass, Shaker Furniture, Wicker, Corkscrews, Barbie Dolls, and so on. Popular engines are Yahoo (yahoo.com), Web Crawler (webcrawler.com), Infoseek (infoseek.com), Lycos (lycos.com), and others. These services are typically free, being supported by advertisers. Try them all; you'll get different results, then use whichever is best for you.

Do not assume that because it's on a computer it has to be true. There are legitimate enterprises, services, and markets online, but there are also scams. Computers, which are machines, do not have the human propensity of lying, but sometimes the people who enter information into computers lie, mislead, and deceive. Much dishonest, unsavory information and graphics appear on the computer screen. GIGO (garbage in garbage out). So be forewarned and look at the screen with a skeptical eye.

Experienced computer buffs know that the contributors to this international network are constantly changing. What you find out there today may be gone, reorganized, altered, or wearing a new face tomorrow. Keep abreast of the changing scene by making use of the up-to-date offerings in bookstores and libraries. Some are designed for newcomers to "computer-dom," and some are more advanced. Here are examples of a few "getting started" reference works, written in understandable layman's terms.

- *Advertising on the Internet*, by Zeff and Aronson, Wiley Computer Publishing.
- *Internet and World Wide Web Simplified*, by IDG Books Worldwide.
- *The Internet & World Wide Web* — the Rough Guide, by Angus J. Kennedy, The Penguin Group.
- *PCs for Dummies*, by Dan Gookin, IDG Books Worldwide.
- *PCs in Plain English*, by Bryan Pfaffen Berger, MIS Press.

Now that you have learned something about identifying, understanding, and evaluating your accumulated possessions, your next step is figuring out how to go about selling or otherwise disposing of them.

Consider first the feasibility and advisability of the charitable donation route as discussed in the next chapter.

CHAPTER FIVE

HOW TO DONATE PROPERTY TO CHARITY

" . . . give and give/Because the throb of giving's
sweet to bear"
    —Dorothy Parker

CAST YOUR BREAD UPON THE WATERS

As you review various options for disposing of your
assorted possessions, don't overlook the opportunity of realizing a good tax advantage by donating your articles to a charitable organization instead of selling them. The amount of this
benefit will depend upon the breakdown of the deductions
you claim on your tax return in relation to your gross income.

It is up to you to record and provide certain data to your
financial adviser, who will explain how this procedure works
for you. Read on for a general overview and explanation of
the way this is done.

The information presented in this chapter comes from ON
HIGH—the IRS law as of the most recent update available at
the time this book was written. It is provided as a general
guideline for weighing how advisable it may be for someone
in your situation to make charitable donations. Detailed calcu-
lations and special factors that apply to your personal circumstances should be discussed and worked out with the help of
legal and financial experts.

This segment of the book discusses three significant subjects
that will affect your donation: what organizations may qualify
to be recipients of your largesse; what kinds of articles may be
donated; and how the articles are evaluated.

ELIGIBLE DONEE ORGANIZATIONS

The beneficiaries of your donation must be one or more of
the following:

A. Community chests, corporations, trusts, funds, or foundations organized or created in or under the laws of the United
States or its subdivisions. They must be designed and operated exclusively for any of the following purposes:

Religious
Educational
Charitable
Scientific
Literary
Prevention of cruelty to children or animals

B. War veterans organizations.

C. Domestic fraternal organizations operating under the lodge system if used for any of the purposes listed under A above.

D. Certain nonprofit cemetery companies except those organized and intended for care of a lot or crypt.

E. The United States or any of its subdivisions if your contribution is to be used solely for public purposes.

Other charities may qualify under certain circumstances. If you have one in mind, consult your tax adviser to determine its eligibility.

When considering where to donate your possessions, do not overlook museums, libraries, universities, historical and

Three unusual postcards showing landmarks in England and Singapore.

genealogical societies, recreation and sports halls of fame, and medical research foundations.

Among the articles that are welcomed and deeply appreciated by such groups and organizations are architects' drawings, mythical maps, medical treatises and equipment, artistic old valentines, vintage photographs of local scenes and personalities, unusual rare picture postcards, and hobby collections. Such mementos and ephemera are often worth much more for their cultural, educational, and historical significance than they would bring in a sale to the general public.

The rare Kodak Medalist camera was designed and produced in the 1940s for the professional photographer. It is in great demand by serious camera buffs who value it in the hundreds of dollars.

Here is a good case in point: A collection of annotated sheet music that had been used for performances held in an old landmark burlesque house was highly prized and appreciated for its historic value by the music department of a major library.

Consider, then, how the following articles would be welcomed by specific eligible organizations and societies.

• You have accumulated an assortment of military medals, ribbons, and awards from historical military campaigns. Imagine how eager the Smithsonian Institution or various national veterans organizations would be to receive such artifacts and place them on permanent display.

• You have a collection of vintage baseball uniforms, caps, and game T-shirts. What a prize this would be for the National Baseball Hall of Fame and Museum.

• Your large assortment of elaborate Victorian wicker furniture has long been gathering dust in your basement. It would be a fine acquisition for the Renwick Gallery of the National Museum of American Art, whose curator recognizes the importance of such vintage furniture and accessories as a true art form of the period.

The following institutions in Rochester, New York, have provided criteria that measure their needs and interests. These examples are offered as an indication of what other organizations throughout the country are looking for, based upon their own areas of specialization.

The Rochester Museum and Science Center: It is interested more in the well-documented story an item can tell than in its beauty, rarity, or dollar value—it seeks particularly articles relating to the Erie Canal; antebellum railroads; and Susan B. Anthony, Frederick Douglass, and other nationally renowned personalities from the area.

Strong Museum: It is currently seeking objects that document immigration trends, especially the articles that immigrants brought with them from Eastern Europe, Southeast Asia, and the former Soviet Union.

George Eastman House: It would like to have items representing technology of motion pictures, photography, and movie posters. For example, it is interested in prototype cameras that never went into widescale production and, in particular, the original, preferably unopened, packaging for camera-related products.

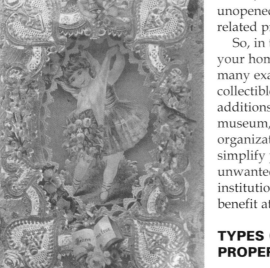

So, in the familiar rooms of your home you will probably find many examples of artifacts and collectibles that would be ideal additions to the exhibitions of a museum, university, or research organization. What a good way to simplify your life—donate your unwanted articles to a worthy institution while reaping a tax benefit at the same time.

TYPES OF DONATED PROPERTY

The following kinds of property can be claimed as charitable donations upon acceptable evaluation and appraisal:

Because they are fragile and delicate, few vintage valentines survive intact to be admired and treasured for the artistic folk art that they are. This typical Victorian specimen dated 1881 is filled with lace and has soft pastel coloring.

• Household goods and apparel: furniture, appliances, designer clothes and accessories, linens, furs.

- Jewelry and unset gems.
- Paintings, antiques, art objects.
- Collections: rare books, stamps, coins, autographs, guns, dolls, antique valentines, and any other articles that have collector value.
- Cars, boats, aircraft.

HOW TO EVALUATE AND OBTAIN DOCUMENTATION

Your tax benefit is calculated on the basis of the fair market value of the property on the date it is donated. Therefore, you should record all factors that will help to determine your article's value on the open market. These include its current cost or selling price; demand for and sales of comparable items; replacement cost; and opinions of experts.

Chantilly lace designer dress lined in silk, handmade in the early 1950s.

- Household goods and apparel: If you plan to donate rare or antique furniture, fine lace or linens, precious furs, or designer clothes and accessories, you should have these items examined and evaluated by specialists who are competent in judging such objects (used, ordinary household effects have little or no market value).

- Jewelry and unset gems: This category is so specialized that it is necessary to get an evaluation from a credentialed jewelry specialist or connoisseur. His report should describe the style of the item; the perfection, cut, and setting of the gemstone; and whether the piece is now in fashion. If it is not, the statement should indicate the possibility of having it redesigned, recut, or reset to make it more marketable. The stone's weight, coloring, brilliance, and flaws, if any, should be noted. Sentimental attachment has no value, but if you can furnish provenance, meaning evidence that it had belonged to a famous person, its value may be enhanced (see pp. 70-72 for a discussion of provenance).

PAINTINGS, ANTIQUES, SCULPTURE, AND OTHER ART OBJECTS

For a single artpiece valued at between $20,000 and $50,000, you must attach a copy of the signed appraisal to your tax return. You may be asked to provide a color photograph of the object.

For an item valued at $50,000 or more, you should ask the IRS to send you a "Statement of Value" form to be completed before filing the return. Call your IRS District Office for further explanations and instructions.

Physical condition and any restoration of antiques and art weigh heavily in analyzing their value and must be disclosed in the appraisal. An antique in damaged condition or missing its "original brasses," for example, is worth far less than a similar piece in mint, unaltered, complete condition.

Individuals contributing art objects to a charity stand to benefit the most if they donate capital gain property. This is property that does not provide an income and that has been owned for the specified length of time, usually at least one year. Artists cannot benefit from this tax law by donating their own work, the reason being that the IRS considers it to be income producing, not capital gain, property while owned by its creator. Neither can art dealers qualify for these tax reduction benefits because they too sell art in order to generate income.

When the artist or dealer donates a work of art to charity, the tax deduction is limited to the cost of the artpiece to the donor. This means that the artist is allowed to deduct only the cost of the materials he used and the dealer only the amount he paid to the artist.

COLLECTIONS

Of the hundreds of article types that people collect, the most popular and valuable are stamps, coins, dolls, figurines, rare books, guns, phonograph records, natural history items, baseball cards, cameras, limited edition articles, and comic books.

Dealer price lists, specialized catalogs, auction results, and collector club periodicals are some of the sources of market value of specific collectibles. When citing these published values, use the current edition and give the date when the item brought the specified price.

In addition to traditional museums, foundations, and historical societies, consider some of the following little known, newer organizations; these would be qualified to receive certain collections owing to their educational, literary, and scientific activities and purposes:

The Houston, Texas, Police Museum
The Salem Witch Museum, Salem, Massachusetts
The Schieles Museum of Natural History in Gastonia, North Carolina
The Lock Museum of America, Terryville, Connecticut
The U.S. Military History Institute, Carlyle, Pennsylvania
The International Space Hall of Fame, Alamogordo, New Mexico
The Heye American Indian Foundation, New York, New York

During the Salem Witch Trials of 1692, fear and superstition led to hundreds of accusations, trials, and executions of innocent, ordinary citizens for the crime of witchcraft. The Salem Witch Museum provides education, exhibits, and dramatizations for history buffs.

STAMPS

Most libraries have catalogs or other reference books that report the publisher's estimates of values. Generally, two price levels are shown for each stamp—postmarked and not postmarked. Stamp dealers have up-to-date values of their stock in trade and can be relied upon to deliver honest appraisals.

COINS

The *Red Book* by R. S. Yeoman has historically been an annual coin price guide utilized by dealers, traders, and collectors. Your coin collection should have a direct, hands-on analysis by a numismatic specialist because age, rarity, condition, and demand—important factors influencing market value—are not usually within the ken of the layman. The same edition of a coin can differ in value by hundreds, even thousands of dollars, according to its relative standing in the A.N.A. (American Numismatic Association) grading scale. Its ratings range from Poor to Good to Fine to Uncirculated to Mint, and ultimately to Proof.

By way of example, a 1919 Liberty Walking half dollar is appraised at about $5 in Good condition, $60 if Very Fine, and as much as $625 if in Mint condition.

BOOKS

The value of a book is usually determined by looking up sales of comparable books and adjusting for variations in condition, appealing features, and other characteristics. It is recommended that this research and analysis be done by a specialized expert/appraiser.

Book dealers are apt to focus on certain special categories such as Americana, scientific and medical classics, Bibles, foreign imports, and other particular categories. A book that is very old or very rare is not necessarily very valuable. Condition is a very important factor: A book suffers substantial downgrading due to a missing page, a loose binding, stains, tears, foxing, or other flaws. Other factors that affect value are the type and condition of the binding (leather, cloth, paper), page edges, and illustrations. The original dust jacket adds a great deal to the value.

First edition modern books, even if they are merely ephemeral popular fiction, are so sought after that certain ones may even outvalue many eighteenth and nineteenth century classics. For example, a good condition first edition of Tom Clancy's *Hunt for Red October* has been reportedly evaluated at $500 or more, and *Catcher in the Rye* by J. D. Salinger was appraised at $4,000 to $6,000.

Unusual photographs, illustrations, or other attractive artwork will enhance the value of books. But the pictures themselves are sometimes worth more on their own than the entire book is worth. That is why many nineteenth century books of flower or other botanical prints, for example, have been taken apart and the prints sold separately.

AUTOGRAPHS, MANUSCRIPTS, DIARIES, ETC.

When these items are handwritten, or at least signed by famous people, they are often in high demand and worth a lot of money. The writings of unknowns may also be of substantial value if they are of unusual historical or literary significance. Signatures that had been excised from letters or other documents usually have little or no value. However, complete sets of such signatures of U.S. presidents or other dignitaries are sought after.

A signed Babe Ruth photograph was offered at $1,900, and a signed John Lennon postcard was appraised at $985. Even autographs of infamous villains are valuable; a signature of Adolph Hitler under a poster-size award given to a German factory in 1943 brought $3,500 a few years ago.

CARS, BOATS, AIRCRAFT

If you donate a vehicle, boat, or airplane to a qualified organization, you must establish its current fair market value. Certain commercial firms and trade organizations publish monthly or seasonal guides commonly called "Blue Books." These catalogs list dealer sales or average prices for certain model years in different regions of the country. Prices apply to each make, model, and year of used cars, trucks, boats, recreational vehicles, and aircraft on the market.

These published guides also provide adjustments to estimates that take into consideration extra or unusual equipment, unusually high or low mileage, and exceptionally good physical condition.

The prices in these guides are not considered or accepted as official appraisals. But they do offer guidelines for making an appraisal, and they quote figures to compare with current sales and offerings in your area at certain times of the year. These publications are sometimes available at a bank, credit union, or finance company.

Except for inexpensive small boats, the valuation of a boat should be based on an appraisal given by a marine surveyor who can assess its physical condition, which is critical to its monetary value.

ADVISORY

You donate your car to a local high school for use by students studying automobile repair. Your credit union quoted its "Blue Book" value at $1,600 in good condition. However, an examination by repair shops and used car dealers reveals that it needs extensive repairs and could bring $750 in its current condition. You may use $750 not $1,600 as its fair market value. Also, bear in mind that you can deduct your donations only in the year that you actually made them.

You may need to identify and locate experts who specialize in specific, unique items or collections. A good source is the current official Museums Directory of the American Association of Museums, which lists museums by state and by category.

QUALIFIED APPRAISALS

(See pp. 93-101 for a full discussion of the appraising profession and appraisal associations.)

For a donation that would effectuate a deduction of more than $5,000, you must obtain a qualified appraisal and attach its summary (not the appraisal itself) to the income tax return. If you donated art worth $20,000 or more, the complete signed appraisal must accompany the return.

Generally, with certain exceptions as spelled out in IRS Publication No. 561, an appraisal that is paid for based on a percentage of the appraised value of the property is prohibited. (For a detailed explanation of how appraisal costs are arrived at, see pp. 97-100.)

A qualified appraisal must include the following information:

• A description of the property that will constitute clear evidence that the article appraised is the article donated.

• The physical condition of any tangible property.

• The date (or expected date) of contribution.

• Any agreement entered into by or on behalf of the donor relating to the use, sale, or other disposition of the donated item(s).

• The name, address, and taxpayer ID number of the appraiser.

• The qualifications of the appraiser who signs the appraisal, including his background, experience, education, and any membership in professional appraisal associations.

• A statement by the signer that the appraisal was prepared for income tax purposes.

• The date or dates when the property was valued.

• The appraised fair market value on the date or expected date of the contribution.

• The method used to determine fair market value, such as the income approach; the comparable sales or market data approach; or the replacement costs less depreciation approach.

• The specific basis for the valuation, such as any documented comparable sales transaction.

Appraisals of art objects — paintings in particular — should include the following information:

• A complete description of the object, including size, subject matter, medium used, name of the artist (or ethnic culture or origin), and approximate date when created.

• Cost, manner, and date of acquisition.

• A history of the item, including proof of authenticity.

• A photograph of a size and quality that fully shows the object, preferably a 10" x 12".

• The facts on which the appraisal was based, such as sales of comparable works by the artist, particularly on or around the valuation date; quoted prices in dealers' catalogs of the artist's works or works of other artists of comparable stature; a record of any exhibitions at which that specific art object had been displayed; the economic state of the art market at the time of valuation, particularly with respect to the specific property; and the standing of the artist in his profession and in the particular school or time period.

NUMBER OF APPRAISALS NEEDED:
   A separate qualified appraisal is required for each individual item. One appraisal will suffice for a group of similar items contributed in the same year, but all the required information must be provided for each separate item in the group.

QUALIFIED APPRAISERS:
   A qualified appraiser is one who declares on the appraisal summary that he/she . . .

• represents himself or herself to the public as an appraiser or regularly performs appraisals.

• is qualified to make appraisals of the type of property being valued because of his or her qualifications described in the appraisal.

• is not an excluded individual. (Excluded individuals are described on p. 10 of IRS publication 561, which lists various situations or relationships which could have a negative impact on the impartiality of the appraisal.)

• understands the penalty for intentionally overstating the value of the property.

   To be considered qualified, the appraiser must also complete Part III of Section B (Form 8283), entitled Noncash Charitable Contributions.

RECORDS TO KEEP:
   When donating property to an organization, you should obtain and keep a receipt from the recipient showing the name

of the charitable, qualified organization; the date and location where the contribution was made; and a description of the item(s) donated. Your own backup records should include, in addition:

• the fair market value of the property at the time of the contribution and how you figured that value. If it was determined by appraisal, you should also keep a signed copy of the appraisal.

• the terms of any conditions attached to the gift of property.

Depending upon how complicated your personal situation is, other records and documentation may be required, and certain forms may have to be filled out and submitted with your return.

You should discuss these possible requirements with your accountant or tax adviser early on so that you have time to do the necessary research and paperwork well in advance of filing time.

AN ALTERNATIVE IDEA

Other than an outright, direct donation to a particular charitable organization, you may want to investigate the benefits of establishing a Charitable Remainder Trust as a method of reducing your tax liability. This involves transferring certain listed securities, cash, or tangible assets to a designated Trust to be held and managed under the terms spelled out. The Trust pays you an annuity for the duration. Upon your death, the Trustee distributes the principal and income in the account to the Charity named in the instrument. This arrangement entitles you to a Federal Income Tax deduction for a portion of the value of your gift. Consult your financial counselor about the details and technicalities of this procedure.

After giving careful consideration to the charitable donation option, you may decide to sell your possessions after all. Read on to learn about various ways to sell.

CHAPTER SIX

HOW TO USE AVENUES FOR SELLING

"You need not hang up the grape ivy branch over the wine that will sell."
— Maxim No. 968 of Pablilius Syrus, ca. 42 B.C.

Successfully selling or otherwise disposing of a lifetime accumulation of treasures is harder than gathering them — that had been done over a period of years, usually in a joyful, impulsive manner. Now what is needed to part with our beloved heirlooms and relics is firm, determined action, sometimes in the face of emotional and/or economic stress.

There are various ways to go about marketing your possessions. Each has its advantages and drawbacks. The options are discussed here, one by one, in detail. The route you take will depend upon many factors — your available time; your experience; your patience, energy, and endurance level; the kinds of articles to be disposed of; and the professional and physical assistance you can enlist to help you.

If you own recently retired limited edition collectibles, you will be entering a so-called secondary market. Like any other economic marketplace, it is subject to supply/demand fluctuations. If your piece was issued in a very small edition, and is popular and in strong demand, you'll find ready buyers. On the other hand, if the item was produced in large runs and is not outstanding, as is the case with most limited editions, it will take a long time, and you will probably have to settle for way below your original purchase price.

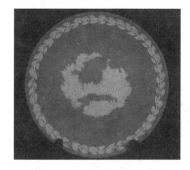

This rare first-edition Wedgwood Christmas plate, "Windsor Castle," made its debut in 1969.

More information is available in "The Collectibles Market Guide and Price Index," published by the Collectors Information Bureau (CIB). Call them at 847-842-2200 for two secondary market quotes on your item.

This chapter provides a variety of selling avenues and techniques for you to consider. You may decide to use a combination of methods. Think over their pros and cons and use your best judgment.

A. DIRECT ADVERTISING

TELL THE WORLD ABOUT IT

You could get a good pay-off from the investment of a few dollars in ads in newspaper and periodical classifieds, antique and collectibles publications, and popular consumer magazines. Following are just a few mass-market magazines that have large circulations of readers who would very likely be interested in your saleables: *Antique Trader Weekly, Yankee, McCalls, Good Housekeeping, Cappers, Family Circle,* and *NY/PA Collector Monthly.* Many more publication possibilities will probably occur to you.

Ads can take various forms: They can be inexpensive two or three liners; larger, more detailed compositions accentuated with bold face type; or elaborate, costly display creations. Look at various ads in print and see which ones catch your attention and why.

Consider placing small ads in a specialty magazine that deals with trading in specific categories of privately owned, marketable articles. This option would probably generate more direct sales than a more costly ad in a general magazine. There are many such periodicals out there that have large, loyal readerships who are potential buyers of exactly what you want to sell. Consider, for example:

Three hand-made quilts — Amish Diamonds, Dahlia, and Double Wedding Ring — are examples of artistic handicraft by skillful, dedicated needleworkers.

Quilters Newsletter Magazine
741 Corporate Circle, Suite A
Golden, CO 80401-5622

Classic Toy Trains
Kalmbach Publishing Co.
21027 Crossroads Circle
Waukesha, WI 53187

Teddy Bear Review
170 Fifth Ave.
New York, NY 10010

Tuff Stuff Guide to Sports Cards & Collectibles
1974 E. Parham Rd.
Richmond, VA 23228

Doll World
306 E. Parr Rd.
Berne, IN 4671

As you peruse published classifieds, you will find that the "Wanteds" far outnumber the "For Sales." Look them over carefully in order to spot seekers of just what you are selling. This is an easy way of reaching and negotiating with a prospective purchaser—at his expense, for he placed the ad!

Do not overlook another possibility: People advertising to sell are very often also buying, so "For Sale" ads could lead you to potential purchasers. For example, a dealer in or collector of Carnival glass may have a supply of duplicates of a particular pattern and is advertising to sell the surplus. But think of this: He could very well turn out to be interested in buying certain other Carnival models that he lacks and that you have. So give him a call and see what kind of mutually satisfactory business you can negotiate.

Here are a couple of "insider" tips that may help you with your advertising plans:

Some magazines offer special discounted rates for unfilled leftover ad space, sometimes called "scrap." They will insert your ad when there's room for it, with no commitment on their part as to when it will appear. To find out about placing scrap advertising, call the magazine and ask to speak to an advertising representative.

This very old iridescent gold Carnival bowl with green stem and base was made by Northwood and inscribed with the "N" mark.

One of the magazine industry's best kept secrets is that advertising terms and prices are often negotiable, especially right before the magazine is printed and there is still space waiting to be filled.

B. MAIL ORDER

USE UNCLE SAM'S PONY EXPRESS

Offering your articles through the mail is a good way of marketing small items that are easy to pack and ship like postcards, spoons, baseball cards, thimbles, sheet music, and other light-weight, compact articles. The best items to sell this way are desirable, easy-to-describe pieces. Among successful mail-order sellers are Depression glass, campaign buttons, vintage fountain pens, World's Fair and Exposition memorabilia, and

Hummel figurines. Large, bulky items are almost impossible to sell by mail order unless they will be picked up by the buyer.

The first thing to do if you take this route is to obtain lists of potential customers to approach with your offerings. There are services that are in the business of designing and selling mailing lists. In your local telephone Yellow Pages you can find list brokers who will do the research and compile a list of consumers chosen on the basis of their interest in your specific products.

This approach, however, is time-consuming, will cost you money, and the results are uncertain. Make sure if you contract for this service that you find out as much as possible about the track-record and reputation of the list broker and know exactly what you are paying for.

You can probably have better and quicker results by developing and implementing a mailing list yourself. What you want to do is target people who would conceivably be in the market for the items you want to sell.

For example, you want to thin out your collection of Hummel figurines. What could be a better mailing list than members of the Hummel Collectors Club, Inc.? How do you reach them? At the following Club address:

> The M.I. Hummel Club
> Goebel Plaza, Rte. 31 P.O. Box 11
> Pennington, NJ 08534

There are at least two more Hummel Collector associations to contact, namely:

> Hummel Collectors Club, Inc.
> P.O. Box 257
> Morrisville, PA 19067

> Tampa Area M.I. Hummel Club
> P.O. Box 3
> Lutz, FL 33549

Approach these organizations to see if they would help you reach their membership or share any other information or advice with you.

If your collection is glass insulators, your best market is members of the National Insulators Ass'n; if corkscrews, the

International Correspondence of Corkscrew Addicts, and on and on. These and practically all other collector clubs are listed in:

> *Maloney's Antiques and Collectibles Resource Directory*
> by David J. Maloney, Jr.
> Antique Trader Books

For purposes of the mail offering, prepare a complete numbered list of every Hummel figurine (or cookie jar, or souvenir spoon, or antique flask, or whatever) that you have. Describe each one in detail, including size; color; hallmarks; condition, including defects; and asking price.

Unless the article is very rare and in strong demand, imperfect condition is a deterrent. However, certain items may be wanted for parts, such as radio and television sets, slot and arcade machines, model railroad cars, musical devices, clocks and watches, and certain mechanical objects.

In mail solicitations, you will greatly increase your chances of making a sale by including with your list: photographs, sketches, or photocopies or rubbings of, for example, your collection of rare head vases. The buyer who sees, recognizes, and wants exactly what you have will give you a quicker and probably more favorable response. Include

Empty head vase.

with your list and pictures a letter of introduction with your name, address, zip code, and telephone and/or FAX number. Enclose an SASE (self-addressed stamped envelope) for return of the list of articles and pix or for further correspondence. Some sellers charge a nominal fee for the list, but this is your option.

Head vase with flowers.

When dealing with a prospective buyer, you should

be prepared: Be sure your asking price has been well researched and is verifiable from price guides, auction results, or other sources. Negotiations should boil down to the bottom line, namely the offer below which you will not budge. So have in mind what you will accept after the haggling and bargaining are over. At that point, stand firm but politely and with decorum.

At the time you and the buyer have sealed the transaction with a handshake, a letter, a telephone call, or other commitment, you should be ready with proper contractual documentation. This could be an informal statement with terms of the sale, a printed sales slip, or a formal bill of sale conveying title. Whatever form the paperwork takes, be sure you and the buyer know exactly what it says and that you understand and accept your mutual responsibilities.

SHIPPING

After a sale is made, you will have to pack and ship the item(s) unless pick-up or other arrangements are planned in advance. Wrap the articles carefully. You will be responsible for breakage, so insure all packages. Obtain a check and verify that it is good before you send the articles.

Remember, what you ship belongs to you until the buyer agrees to accept it. Do a good packing job because if an item arrives broken, you have lost a sale AND the item.

To pack a few small, fragile articles, surround them with bubble wrap or "popcorn." Do not use crumpled-up newspaper because the newsprint ink can stain your precious china or other vulnerable treasures. Use a strong outer box, never shoeboxes or other unstable containers. A good choice is a bookbox, which is strong, rigid, and clean. The Post Office is a good source of convenient box sizes at reasonable prices.

Packing china and glassware should not be a problem if you make sure that no two pieces touch. Padding such as bubble pack, Styrofoam sheets, or similar protective material must separate every piece. Lids should be wrapped separately from their bowl or vessel. The pair are apt to chip or break if packed together as a unit. Do not Scotch tape a lid to its bowl; when being pulled off, the tape can cling to and remove the artwork, gilt, or other decoration.

Bubble wrap bags, which come in a variety of sizes, are good containers for shipping large amounts of delicate, breakable articles. Look for them under "Paper Supply" or "Packing" in the Yellow Pages. An even better alternative is to turn over the entire packing and shipping job to PAK MAIL or another such service that guarantees its work.

When shipping a document or other paper item, mail it flat between at least two sheets of heavy cardboard on each surface.

Be sure to arrange to get a return receipt as evidence that the package arrived and was accepted.

C. AUCTIONS

GOING, GOING, GONE!

"These are the letters which Endymion wrote
To one he loved in secret, and apart
And now the brawlers of the auction mart
Bargain and bid for each poor blotted note"
—Oscar Wilde, on the sale by auction of
Keats' love letters

Auctions provide a popular, open marketplace where public, competitive bidding produces fair values for properties being offered for sale. Museums, fine art dealers, celebrities, private collectors, and libraries make a practice of buying and selling at auction.

Purchasing by offering the highest bid is nothing new. Public auctions were common activities thousands of years ago. Herodotus, a Greek writer who was called the father of history, wrote in the fifth century B.C. about the auction of virgins for marriage; bachelors of Babylon scurried to the marketplace to compete for brides at annual auctions. According to some documented accounts, even the Roman Empire was offered at auction when the senators in the first century A.D. legislature could not find a suitable ruler for their then troubled and geographically scattered, unwieldy empire. But this strategy failed because contending armies were battling for control, and conditions were in a state of chaos and upheaval.

Of course the offering of slaves on the auction block is a well-known stigma on our country's tumultuous infancy that will forever haunt us.

Nowadays, using the auction as an avenue for marketing one's possessions is a practical, sensible thing to do. Even if you are not experienced in the ways of the auction business, you can make good use of the services of such establishments. They are available not only to help you sell, but also to provide authenticating and appraising advice. If you have old furniture, unidentified artpieces, bronze figurines, or other mystery items, you will be welcomed by specialists who will provide quick, reliable answers to your questions.

Perhaps your most crucial decision is choosing the auction house that meets your particular needs. A firm that regularly deals in articles similar to yours, or one that has a good sales record in items in your area of collecting, increases the odds that the audience will include serious buyers interested in what you have to offer. A good auction house will also publicize its sale in local newspapers or national publications to notify and attract that largest number of potential buyers.

If you are lucky enough to have some rare Edward Marshall Boehm porcelains to sell, you are sure to get SUPER service from the major auction houses. Such items are in great demand, hard to find, and realize big prices.

Road Runner with horned toad created, designed, and sculptured in hardpaste porcelain by Edward Marshall Boehm. Issued in restricted limited edition in 1968.

Examine antiques magazines and trade papers to find auction house advertisements. Talk to people who have been through this process to get referrals. Check the credit rating of the firm you are considering. If it should go bankrupt, you have small chance of getting the return of your items or the proceeds for those that are sold.

Find out how long the company has been holding sales in this category of objects, how many sales of this sort they conduct per year, and what training their specialists have had. If you can, attend a preview or a sale to see what buyers the company attracts, how the specialists interact with interested potential purchasers, and how well they represent the seller.

Once you have chosen an auction company, you will be asked to sign a contract that outlines the terms of the agreement, including the fees charged for specific services. In most cases, you are responsible for shipping, insurance, catalog photography, and, of course, the auction house's commission. Standard commission rates range from 5 to 25 percent of the sold-at price. Be aware that you may be charged a fee if your property does not sell or is withdrawn from the sale.

Everything is negotiable when dealing with an auction house so always try to get the best "seller" rate. If your items constitute a major profitable sale opportunity for the auction house, you can justifiably ask for extra advertising, preparation and dissemination of an illustrated catalog, even a preview party.

A few days after the sale, the firm should contact you with the amounts your property fetched or to inform you if any of your items failed to sell. Your payment will be the final bid price minus all fees agreed to in the contract. You should expect to receive a check in up to about six weeks. Confirm at the time of the contract signing what the company's payment policy and practice are, so there are no surprises after the sale. If a catalog was produced, you should receive a copy of it along with an addendum showing the final sale results.

You may think, as most people do, that major auction houses deal exclusively with important masterpieces of art, Oriental rugs, vintage furniture, precious jewelry, and other rare treasures. Historically, such valuable articles did comprise their stock in trade. But it is an interesting development that prestigious, discriminating establishments are increasingly dealing with artifacts, heirlooms, curiosities, folk art, and other items that are being collected by ordinary folk. So they will be glad to look at whatever you want to sell and offer their services and expertise.

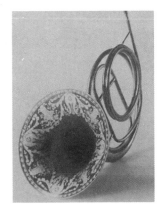

Auction galleries often feature individual sales focusing on weather vanes, dolls, clocks and watches, Americana, or other popular specialties. Your collection of rare musical instruments or daguerreotypes may be good candidates for such a sale if you have a substantial quantity and of fine enough quality that it would be profitable for the firm to invest its resources and personnel in staging such an event.

This orchestral horn made by D. Jahn in Paris ca. 1825 has a beautiful original painted design. It is an example of a rare musical instrument that would be featured in a special auction.

On the other hand, suppose you have only one, or just a few unrelated articles that you want to sell. If your article is portable and you are near a full-service

These cast-iron figural bookends with gilt trim were manufactured in the early 1940s.

auction house, bring it in to be examined. Sotheby Parke Bernet and Christie's are the two largest and give the most comprehensive service. They have qualified experts in a full range of article categories and they furnish free appraisals, advice, and auction arrangements.

If you are able to come to New York and want to seek their help, it would be advisable to make an appointment in advance with the appropriate department. They have specialists in Art Nouveau or Deco, photographs, paperweights, folk art, jewelry, musical instruments, bookends, pre-Columbian art, books and manuscripts, and a full range of collectibles.

Here are the addresses and telephone numbers of these auctioneer giants:

This quarter-plate image on a metal plate, a daguerreotype, is a precursor of the paper photographic print. It is distinguished by its mirror-like reflection and precise detail. Most daguerreotypes were damaged, lost, or melted down for their metal content. Whatever good specimens survive are therefore valuable.

Sotheby Parke Bernet
1334 York Ave.
New York, NY 10021
212-606-7440

Christie's
502 Park Ave.
New York, NY 10022
212-546-1000

If you cannot bring your article in personally, both of these establishments will provide a "preliminary" (without commitment) free appraisal through the mail; all you have to do is send in a clear photograph of your item accompanied by a detailed description (material; dimensions; artist's signature or maker's mark; provenance, if any; condition, including repairs or defects; and when and where the article was acquired).

Find out if there is a large auction house near you that has specialists and offers similar services.

Very old polychrome, hand painted pottery Japanese peasant couple.

Remember and consider the emotional factors that affect the bidding process at an auction (see pp. 71-72). The results depend upon the mood and objectives of the players (bidders) and their interaction at a given time. The final "sold-at" figures become the statistics most often cited as representing actual market demand.

Regulars who attend and participate in auctions are familiar with the lexicon of terms that describe what is going on. For a newcomer to the scene, the jargon may be mystifying. The following glossary will help you understand the scenario:

AUCTION TERMS

Appraisal: The evaluation of an object's monetary worth on the market; most auction houses will provide either a free verbal estimate or a formal, written document for insurance, tax or probate purposes, for which they charge a fee.

Bidding increments: The auctioneer will announce the amount of the increment by which each bid is increased.

Bought in: When a lot does not sell at an auction, the item(s) is "bought in" by the auctioneer, meaning that it remains the property of the owner.

Buyer's premium: A fee paid by the buyer added to the final bid amount, usually 10 percent.

Hammer price: The term used to describe the successful bid.

Knocked down: The fall of the auctioneer's hammer after the final bid; e.g., Lot 6 was knocked down at $1,500.

Lot: An item or group of items offered for sale as a unit.

Order bid: A written or verbal bid executed (offered) on your behalf when you are not present to bid for yourself.

Presale estimate: A range of prices expected to be "fetched" for each lot; this data appears in the catalog, if any.

Provenance: An object's history of ownership.

Seller's reserve: The minimum price agreed upon between the seller and the auction house below which an item will not be sold; i.e., the item will be bought in if the bidding does not reach the reserve price.

RURAL AUCTIONS

There are occasions when auctions are conducted in a barn, a private estate or residence, a store, a warehouse, or any country setting. Tools, furniture, farm machinery, equipment, and various sundries are displayed and sold usually outdoors under a canopy or pavilion or in the open, where rows of folding chairs are often put in place for the comfort of the participants.

If the possessions you wish to sell are located on a farm or in a rural setting, you may find this kind of an auction the best way for you to dispose of them.

In such an auction, there is usually no published catalog or list of items being offered. Instead, a newspaper announcement or distributed flyers may be utilized to publicize a few of the highlights or special desirables. Rural auctions are informal, flexible, and provide an inviting opportunity for visiting or socializing.

Everything imaginable shows up at these country sales. In addition to household furniture and accessories, offerings include quilts, folk art, hooked rugs, old appliances and kitchen utensils, wood-burning stoves, vintage apparel, farm equipment, and, of course, livestock. Even half sets or unmatched dishes, broken tools, torn magazines and books, and rolls of chicken wire will be wanted by someone.

An eminent appraiser had a call from a farmer in the Midwest asking him to evaluate a collection that he did not describe over the phone. He flew a long distance from his eastern headquarters and then drove many more miles to the owner's farm. There he finally was shown the collection to be put on the auction block. It was the accumulation of many years of the farmer's obsession with his hobby: Eighty well-scrubbed amusing out-houses and 100 cast-iron stoves. So there's no telling what kind of merchandise can show up at a country sale.

An early manual meat grinder made by Enterprise is a rare collectible.

For regular, year-round sales in foul as well as fair weather, general or specialized auctions are often held indoors in barns, grange halls, county courthouses, or any large convenient building. In planning such sales, arrangements can be made to have the merchandise transported from estates, farms, or residences to the auction location by the auctioneers and his helpers. The seller would usually be charged a set fee plus, or instead of, a percentage of the gross receipts, which might range from 10 to 30 percent.

Because of the disrepute some country auctioneers have fallen into in recent times, certain states now require that they be officially bonded and licensed. You should check this out before contracting with an auctioneer.

D. DEALERS

A QUICK TURNOVER

Probably the fastest and most convenient way of selling your antiques and collectibles is to call a dealer to come over and make an offer to purchase everything. This could be your best option if you live in a city other than where the property is located, or have inherited a few large pieces, or no longer have an interest in most of these "things," or must move this

A spirited silver-plated horse engraved "Ft. Riley, KAN."

burdensome stockpile as soon as possible. On the other hand, you may have a large number of interesting possessions and lack the time and the resources to make an efficient sales effort.

Before you call a dealer, be sure that you have researched and evaluated each and every item you are selling and that you can negotiate intelligently and successfully.

Since the dealer's travel time will affect his offer, try to find and use a reputable local dealer who can conveniently come to your house, look over your possessions, and work with you towards arriving at a mutually satisfactory price.

When displaying the furniture and accessories you are offering, never give anyone access to your house when you are not there. If possible, make sure at least two people are in the house and have a good vantage point when a potential buyer arrives.

Arrange for the dealer to pay you when he removes the articles or, if a large number of unwieldy items are involved, be prepared with the legalities of shipment, transfer of title, and payment arrangements.

Here is something to bear in mind when selling to local dealers: Set your price with the national market as the target. A favorite ploy you may

An example of Americana folk art, this old-fashioned Wizard manual pencil sharpener was rescued from thousands of sticky little fingers and is treasured for the nostalgic rarity that it is.

encounter is the dealer downgrading the values you have set. He may say, "But those are New York, not 'Countryville' prices." What such entrepreneurs will not admit is that they will take, for example, your Duncan Phyfe table and put it up for sale in a Manhattan auction gallery. A fine, rare antique is just as deserving, and capable of realizing, top price in your town as in a big city.

When selling pieces to a dealer, sell each item individually, not "as a lot." However, a matched, complete collection should be sold as a set, otherwise the choice pieces will be snatched up, leaving you left with the lesser items.

E. COLLECTOR CLUBS

CHECK OUT THESE FRIENDLY EXCHANGES

If you have a supply of a specific collectible category that you are ready to sell, you may be surprised and happy to learn about an eager audience out there seeking those very items. There are scores of collector clubs that concentrate on certain types of articles — thimbles, cufflinks, decoys, beer cans, postcards, lunchboxes, Pez dispensers, cookbooks, mechanical action banks, fishing lures, antique combs, and innumerable other specialty items and memorabilia.

For a nominal fee, you can join the club of your choice and cement relations with your fellow addicts on a social as well as an information sharing basis. If you prefer not to become a member, you can still meet with them, correspond with them, learn about their activities, and attend their meets and special events. Many collector societies produce periodicals and newsletters that publish notices of meetings and conventions, cultural and historical events, exhibitions, and, especially for your purposes, print buying, selling, and trading ads.

For the most comprehensive and best organized list of collector clubs, buyers, restorers, museums, periodicals, and a lot more detailed information, consult Maloney's "Bible" (see p. 131). This preeminent reference work is available in most bookstores and libraries.

The Antique Trader Weekly is America's largest antiques and collectibles marketplace. It contains thousands of "for sale" and "wanted" ads, a regularly updated list of collector books, feature stories, a collector club show and auction calendar, and letters to the editor:

The Antique Trader Weekly
P.O. Box 1050   Dubuque, IA 52004
1-800-531-0880

Another excellent source of information is the *New York/Pennsylvania Collector Monthly*:

The NY/PA Collector Monthly
666 Phillips Rd.   Victor, NY 14564
716-924-4040

Along with illustrated feature articles, this periodical publishes a column announcing meetings and activities of various collector clubs and societies. The following one that appeared recently exemplifies the kind of interchange made possible through conventions, exhibitions, and seminars.

WHITE IRONSTONE ENTHUSIASTS PLAN FOR CONVENTION

"The president of the White Ironstone China Association, Inc., announced details of the group's current annual convention to be held on _____ in Canandaigua, N.Y. The convention will highlight newly researched information on white ironstone miniatures. Members will be able to attend one of three educational workshops. At a swap sale, members may match missing parts and pieces. The evening banquet will be followed by an auction of rare ironstone in mint condition."

Members of collector clubs are often experienced, knowledgeable experts in their field or, on the other hand, they may be novices or part-time, casual participants. All are equally respected and valued by their fellow buffs.

Perusing the activities of collector clubs often leads to interesting information and revelations. Who would imagine that one of the most elite groups of accumulators are among the "chosen" because they are screwy over corkscrews? The International Correspondence of Corkscrew Addicts (ICCA) is hypnotized by this impudent little critter that presumes to uncork a bottle of wine quickly, smoothly, and without crumbling the cork.

Prestigious, austere Christie's of London had an auction in August 1997 of—not priceless Tiffany, antique rugs, precious jewelry, or Oriental art of ancient dynasties—but what is considered the world's largest private collections of bottle uncorking devices. Thousands of unusual corkscrew specimens garnered 192,389 pounds (about 295,000 U.S. dollars), well above the estimated pre-sale total.

This corkscrew addicts' insider society expects its members to be discriminating, judgmental, and totally crazy about their hobby and the unusual models they collect.

Here are the addresses and telephone numbers of the two most important active corkscrew collectors clubs:

International Correspondence of Corkscrew Addicts
20 Fairway Dr.
Stamford, CT 06903
203-968-1925

Canadian Corkscrew
Collectors Club
670 Meadow Wood Rd.
Mississauga, Ontario
L5J 2S6 Canada
905-823-3754

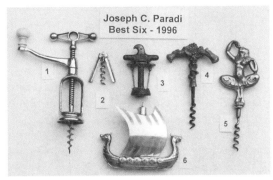

Some of club member Joseph Paradi's most prized corkscrews in his collection.

Another fascinating collectible that has had a centuries-old history and is getting more popular as time goes by is marbles. There are several active clubs whose aggregate membership far surpasses that of most collector societies. These buffs are inspired by the precious materials and artistry of these exquisite globes and equally with the game. Two of the most important marble clubs are:

Marble Collectors Society of America
P.O. Box 222   Trumbull, CT 06611
203-261-3223

National Marble Club of America
440 Eaton Rd.   Drexel Hill, PA 19026
610-622-4444

Some specimens being collected are so rare and so coveted that their prices soar into thousands of dollars. Members consider identification and authentication of marbles serious business as there are reproductions galore on the market.

There are also many thousands of active national and international postcard collectors in dedicated pursuit of unusual, artistic specimens. They belong to the Monumental Postcard Club, the International Postcard Ass'n. Inc., the Deltiologists of America, the Denver

Comic strip marbles sold in the 1930s for 25¢ a box of twelve. Now they are so rare they cost up to $75 each if they can be found.

Sulphides, overlays, clambroths, and other unusual marble specimens command high prices among collectors.

Postcard Club, and the Postcard History Society, among others. Their activities include developing historical and cultural postcard archives, organizing displays and exhibitions, and maintaining trading posts for collectors. They, as well as almost all other collector societies, can be located through *Maloney's Resource Directory* (see p. 131).

(see p. 131).

You may be surprised to learn about sky-rocketing interest in Zippo lighters as an American classic. This little device was created in 1932 and named as a spin-off from the then newly-invented phenomenon, the zipper. The basic design of the Zippo lighter continues unchanged from its original concept, a real accolade for a product that has delivered "matchless" service for almost seventy years.

Not only do Zippos gracefully and faultlessly light cigarettes in wind as well as calm, but they have done yeoman service in time of war, as any G.I. will testify. They have started campfires in European forests and Asian jungles; cooked soup in helmets; served as rescue beacons in open boats; illuminated high-altitude instrument panels in damaged aircraft; and saved lives by stopping bullets.

It stands to reason that the avid Zippo collector can look forward to ever-increasing values for his treasures. The reason: Everything related to smoking, especially vintage, discontinued items, is becoming rare.

> Zippo Collectors Club
> 118 W. 6th Ave.   York, PA 17404

These are but a few examples of the multitude of scholarly collectors who study, respect, and appreciate the objects of their interest. They are lifelong, tireless searchers for their chosen treasures, and the shot of adrenaline they get from a lucky find is proof positive of the therapeutic benefits of this activity.

If you share a common interest in a specific category of collectible with any of these avid buffs and are now in the process of selling all or part of your accumulated stockpile, do communicate with them. You will learn a lot, enjoy a lot, and trade and sell a lot through the contacts made this way.

F. SELLING ON CONSIGNMENT

PUT IT IN WRITING

If you have among your surplus possessions artpieces, antiques, vintage furniture and jewelry, fine artifacts, or even items that seem like trinkets but may be treasures, consider the advantages of selling such objects by consignment. This arrangement, where you are the consignor, means turning over your item(s) to an agent, usually an auction house or a dealer, who will sell the piece at an agreed upon price and charge you a fee for his services. You receive the proceeds and pay the agent an agreed upon commission.

This course of action has two advantages: (1) An expert is selling the item in an established market and (2) You know the proceeds of the sale and the fee you owe the agent.

You measure the desirability of this procedure in terms of certain variables: first is the price you and your agent agree upon. Next is the specific terms of the contract you and your agent execute. Consignment contracts vary according to the practices of each auction house and agent, pursuant of course to your own requirements.

Before choosing the agent, shop around. Compare differences in estimates of value of your article(s); in consignment fees; in additional costs such as insurance, catalog photography, and handling; in advertising arrangements; and in timing and method of payments. Once you have selected your agent, reduce all the terms and conditions of the contract to writing before finalizing it.

Write a full description of your article(s) on the consignment contract. Use the words "mint condition," "flaked paint," "one missing knob," or any other applicable terms. If your item does not sell and you take it back, you will want evidence that it has not been altered or damaged while in the custody of the agent.

As you weigh the respective advantages of consigning with an auction house in contrast with a dealer, you should think about certain factors. Auctions are the ideal avenue if your property is unique, rare, or would benefit from expert hands-on evaluation by a specialist. Let us say, for example, that you have acquired what seems to be a genuine Shaker cobbler bench; or that you have discovered an undocumented work by an early American artist; or that you have clung to a baseball that Mickey Mantle signed for you when you were a kid.

These are the types of articles that may be better marketed by an important auction house that deals regularly with a wide range of artpieces and specialties. If you are turning such items over to a major auction gallery, be patient because such prestigious, conscientious firms often take their time to research, photograph, and catalog each item. This enables them to do the best possible job in promoting and selling your article(s).

NOTE: Everything is negotiable at an auction house if you have a large enough number of desirable, high-demand items to put on the auction block.

You may come to the conclusion that a dealer is your best sales agent for the following reasons: (Dealers may include antique shops, resale shops, creative arts and crafts businesses, used designer apparel shops, and estate disposal services.)

1) The item is marketed to a limited, selected clientele and will not become "dead" as would be expected after an unsuccessful auction sale.

2) You would be apt to get slightly higher prices in antique shops and private galleries consistent with the long-term personal relationships and dealings between the dealer and his outlets.

3) A dealer is in a position to hold out and negotiate for "top dollar." He can price a consigned item higher than a comparable item in his own stock because his capital is not tied up in the consigned item.

4) You can be paid as soon as the sale is consummated.

You must establish in writing that the item will not be sold for under a specific amount and that you will receive all but a determined portion of the proceeds representing the commission. Otherwise, a dealer could take your item anywhere in the country, or world, and sell it for more than you would have any way of knowing. This eventuality is beyond your control — unless you forbid it in your contract.

In sum, if you are willing to submit to the fluctuations of the auction market, can afford to wait for your money, and want a fixed sale date, consign through an auction house. If you have or can establish a good relationship with a reputable dealer and are willing to trade off a specific sale date for potentially greater returns, you may find it better to consign through an art, jewelry, antique, and/or home furnishings dealer.

Pawn shops, used furniture outlets, re-sale shops, and the like are other avenues that often make consignment arrangements for marketing your articles. These businesses are usually small, privately owned enterprises where negotiations and contracts are informal and do not follow a uniform pattern.

If you want to turn your saleables over to such establishments, be careful to check their credit standing, business credentials and reputations, and protect yourself with thorough research.. And by all means participate in negotiating the terms and conditions of the consignment agreement.

Consignment agreements can take different forms, as illustrated by the following examples of documents.

EXHIBIT A

TYPICAL AUCTION CONSIGNMENT AGREEMENT

1. Date of sale: The property described herein will be sold on _____ subject to change without notice in our absolute discretion. We, however, may withdraw any property before sale if we deem it unsuitable for auction for any reason or if we believe you have breached this agreement.

2. Commission: You agree to pay us, and we are authorized to retain from the proceeds of the sale as a commission an amount equal to 10 percent of the final hammer price on each lot sold over $1,000, 15 percent on each lot sold for $1,000 or less, and 25 percent on each lot for $250 or less. Also, it is agreed that 10 percent of the successful hammer price of each lot sold is to be collected by us from the purchaser.

3. Other charges: Packing and shipping charges of _____ will be deducted from the proceeds of the sale. Catalog illustration charges of $50 per illustration will be deducted from the proceeds.

4. Insurance: Unless we have made previous arrangements with you, insurance costs of $1.00 per hundred dollars will be deducted from the proceeds of the sale. If you sustain loss or damage to your property, settlement will be made based on the final median estimate. Our liability to you resulting from loss or damage to any property shall not exceed the above mentioned insurance coverage. In no event will we be liable for damage to glass, frames, or lampshades, regardless of cause.

5. Title: You represent and warrant that the property consigned hereunder is your own unencumbered property and

that you have the right to consign it for sale and that it will be kept free of claims of others so that at the sale good title and interest will pass to the purchaser. If you are consigning the merchandise as fiduciary, you warrant that you are fully authorized to consign the property and agree to assume all of the obligations in this Agreement to the same extent if the undisclosed Seller was acting as principal and will, if required by us, supply any additional documents which we may need.

6. Estimates: The figures set forth in our catalog are estimates only and are not to be deemed a representation by us in any way as to what the property will actually fetch at auction.

7. Reserves: All agreed reserves are set forth on the pre-sale advice which will be mailed to you before the auction. Reserve prices do not include premiums or taxes. You, or any representative designated by you, expressly agree not to bid on the property, it being understood that all bids to protect this reserve will be made by us as your agent. We may sell any property at a price below the reserve provided that we pay you on the settlement date the net amount you would have been entitled to receive had the property been sold for the reserve price. If that property does not reach the agreed reserve and is bought in by us for your account, you agree to pay us a commission of 5 percent of the reserve price and to reimburse us for all "out of pocket" costs incurred by us in connection with your property.

8. Withdrawal of property: You agree that no property may be withdrawn by you after the execution of this Agreement. If you request withdrawal of a lot, you agree to pay us 20 percent of our most recent pre-sale estimate and to reimburse us for all "out of pocket" costs incurred by us.

9. Unsold property: All property which is not sold at auction will be returned to you, at your expense, unless the property is reconsigned.

EXHIBIT B

RESELLERS, INC.
CONDITIONS OF CONSIGNMENT

We accept your new and nearly new, current style clothes. We accept clothes that are free from stains, missing buttons, rips, holes, and must be in style.

Commissions are on a 50/50 split. Any item not sold after 60 days will be reduced by 50%. After 90 days any item not sold must be pulled by the consignor. All unsold items left after 90 days will become the property of Alterations.

We reserve the right to price all items.
We have a 2 week layaway. If an article of yours is not in stock, please ask, it may be on layaway.

After one year any inactive account will be canceled. YOU MUST CALL US. WE WILL NOT CALL YOU.

I, the undersigned, hereby consign to Re-sellers for a minimum of 60 days but not to exceed 90 days these items.

I understand that Re-sellers assumes no responsibility for lost or damaged merchandise by fire, theft, accident or any other cause as this is a public store.

I understand and accept the terms of this agreement

_____ date _____

G. ESTATE, GARAGE, YARD, AND MOVING SALES

THE NEIGHBORHOOD MARKET

Consider various methods whereby you can market your surplus goods within your neighborhood.

1) Use a liquidator or estate professional: These specialists advertise their services in the Yellow Pages and in weekly newspaper sales listings. They contract to handle your entire clearing-out process—advertising, pricing and tagging, security, permits, signs, staff, and special problems or conditions. You pay them an agreed upon percentage of the proceeds.

Following are the preparations involved in contracting with a liquidator: Have a complete up-to-date list of all the items being sold; it helps if you can provide documentation such as sales slips, appraisals, or other identifying or evaluating information. Be sure to obtain and verify references of the people you hire; they will be in your home, handling your money, and the proceeds you receive are based upon their records. If feasible, work with a written contract that specifies your respective tasks and responsibilities, and the amount and terms of the fees.

Be sure your homeowners insurance is in effect and will cover damage or loss to your premises, possessions, workers, and buyers.

Arrange in advance and put it in writing that the unsold pieces should be (1) sent to a specified address (2) picked up, or (3) given to your favorite charity (see Chapter Five for the tax advantage of a donation). Your house should be left as "broom clean" as possible.

If you have only a few items or certain fine jewelry or artwork to sell, it may be a good idea to give your agent permission to place them in a sale of another agent who specializes in such categories. Be sure to record all the details of this arrangement.

Many of us may have a strong emotional attachment to our personal possessions. If you feel this way, do NOT attend the event. You may become upset and may even interfere unintentionally with the sale and discourage a potential customer. If you have special ties to some pieces and would be distraught if you were not offered what you think they are worth, set a price and specify that they not be sold below that figure without your consent. Be ready to cut prices on the last day of the sale to dispose of what is left.

2) Do it yourself: Any motivated, energetic seller can handle a garage or house sale. There are books telling exactly how to do it in many libraries and bookstores. Before proceeding with any plans or arrangements, check with the local police and authorities to learn about permits, parking, signs, sales tax, and other important considerations. Some condominiums, housing developments, and towns prohibit such sales. Research your local laws; it is illegal in some states to sell guns, whiskeys, parts of endangered animals, gambling devices, used mattresses, and other named articles.

Observe some local sales and notice their physical set-up, their security measures, their tagging and pricing practices, and their price reduction policy, if any. Your local newspaper may offer a free garage sale kit containing directions and signs. And by all means, advertise. Place a notice in your neighborhood newspaper and hang small flyers on posts and in grocery stores after obtaining permission.

3) Arrange a group sale: Get together with your friends and neighbors and organize a big cooperative garage, yard, or house sale. Choose the most accessible, conspicuous address, preferably near a major thoroughfare and with convenient parking space. Review and agree among yourselves upon methods of bookkeeping and payment beforehand to avoid confusion and misunderstanding about who owned which items.

Price and tag your own items and be sure you are all in accord about the price cutting procedures. This ground effort works best if at least one participant has had previous experience with this type of sale.

ALERT

Theft is the biggest problem for an inexperienced house or garage sale vendor. Be suspicious of the following items that are brought in: Large receptacles like shopping bags, purses, unbuttoned raincoats, or roomy open bags.

If possible, have shoppers check all large items and coats at the door. If the sale is in the garage, do not let anyone enter the house. If it is in the house, try to have one salesperson in each open room to be an observer. Be sure each sales slip is written by the salesperson assigned to the room where that item is. For example, have one sales helper in charge of all linens and clothes and have all such stock in one room.

Keep small valuable items like jewelry in a special container near the cashier. All money should be paid in one place, preferably on a table that faces the exit door. Watch the money box or cash register. If it is a large sale with many valuable items, it might be a good investment to hire an off-duty policeman.

Be sure all doors other than the selected exit door are locked. Tape shut all cabinets and doors to rooms that do not contain merchandise for sale. If the sale goes on for more than one day, make sure before leaving at night that all windows and doors are locked. Burglars have been known to "case" a sale, open a window, and return that night to make off with articles, knowing the house is unoccupied.

It would be wise to inform the local police of the sale so they can put an extra watch on the house at night. After all, you did place an ad in the paper announcing an empty house filled with merchandise.

Expect to have some losses. Incredible things have happened. Price tags have been switched; boxes filled with unpaid for items are removed; and one saleslady even had her lunch stolen because she had placed it in a gaudy, tempting department store shopping bag!!

H. FLEA MARKETS

WHERE EVERYTHING SELLS

The term "flea market" comes from the French *marche aux puces* (market of fleas), referring to the admission that the bedding and clothing sold at these earliest outdoor marketplaces

were apt to be infested with these critters. American tourists imported the name after World War II and it became coin of the realm.

Let's say you have sold most of your important furniture, antiques, heirlooms, and collectibles through the various avenues described. Now you have a quantity of miscellaneous leftovers you want to get rid of at the best price, of course. Consider the flea market route.

This is not only an excellent marketplace. It also serves as a mecca that attracts people who want to look around, do some walking, socialize, get fresh air, and find surprise discoveries and bargains. More people go to flea markets than to concerts, baseball games, golf courses, or theaters. A flea market is big business—a showplace, bazaar, and museum for vintage artifacts and relics of bygone times.

Flea markets have been heady entertainment in Europe since the Middle Ages or earlier and in the United States since Colonial times. Their fascination is universal and irresistible. An outing to rummage through other people's cast-offs is an exciting activity enjoyed by hordes of men, women, and even family groups. Flea marketers are a sophisticated, eclectic breed: Rural and urban, rich and poor, young and old, discriminating collectors and haphazard bargain hunters.

In terms of popularity, physical size, and numbers, and volume of business, flea markets rank No. 1 among sales arenas. Flea markets attract passionate, energetic, savvy, determined shoppers.

So why not avail yourself of this potential market for your sundries? And have a good time in the process!

There are two ways you can sell in a flea market: Do it yourself or use a dealer.

1) You're On Your Own: Label and arrange your items and set up your own booth. If you have time and energy, enjoy crowds and socializing, and don't mind packing and unpacking, this is a good idea. Check your local newspapers, the Yellow Pages, and antiques and collectibles newsletters for listings and schedules.

Visit a few and inquire about how to rent space and what the practices and requirements are. Notice how the tables are arranged, if they are covered in case of rain, and what the hours are. See if there is a lunch stand on the premises.

What to bring:
- A folding chair.
- A closed box to hold money.
- Newspapers and bubble wrap; shopping bags.
- Rain gear, sun hat, sunglasses.
- A tape measure and loupe for the convenience of a potential buyer.
- Receipt forms.
- Pencil or pen and paper.
- Toilet paper.
- A first-aid kit.

Recruit an assistant to help and to spell you at your post. Never leave your booth unattended. You may want time out to eat, go to the rest room, or visit other booths. You are committed to stay the full day, regardless of how much or how little business you are doing and regardless of the weather. You must price the items, keep records, and give receipts.

Learn the state sales tax regulations. Find out whether you need a resale license. Again, in some states it is illegal to sell slot machines, guns, liquor, pelts and parts of endangered species, and certain other things. So do your homework in advance.

2) Sell to flea market dealers: If you intend to approach a dealer in a flea market with the proposition that he purchase your articles for resale, this is what to do:

Take clear photographs of your stock and record on their backs the size, marks, any other documentation or interesting history of each piece. You might also include a price, but write it in a code that only you can interpret.

Find a dealer who sells items similar to yours and wait to talk to him when his booth is empty; do not start a selling discussion when he is busy with a customer.

When you have the attention of the dealer, ask him if he is interested in buying, then show him the pictures. Or offer to show him the articles you have in the trunk of your car. Dealers are usually interested because it is harder for them to find good items to buy than to sell what they have. Most dealers will expect you to set the price. Your technique is to add 20 percent to the lowest price you will accept and negotiate from there. Remember — the dealer works on the premise that he will sell the item for twice what he pays you.

Sometimes the dealer will not want your items, but if you establish a good relationship with him, he may suggest a customer, another dealer, or a collector who is on the premises.

Be discreet. Don't expect a free appraisal. Know the market value of your articles.

WHERE THE FLEA MARKETS ARE

To list the thousands of gigantic seasonals, hundreds of smaller monthlies and weeklies, and finally all the ad hoc roadsiders would be a massive, endless and ever-changing undertaking.

If time and movability are limited and restricted, check the local newspapers and trade publications for announcements and particulars of nearby sales. This way you can sort out and examine the information and plan your strategy accordingly.

If you are flexible enough to be able to plan a long trip, consult the following national guides:

- *Clark's Flea Market USA* (Clark's Publications, 2156 Cotton Patch Lane, Milton, FL 32570).

- *The Great American Flea Market Directory* (Cranbrook House, Saginaw, MI 48608).

- *The Official Directory to U.S. Flea Markets* (House of Collectibles, Division of Ballantine Books, NYC 10022).

To select the right flea market for your purposes would depend upon your specific goals; how much time, money, and energy you have for traveling; your mode of travel; how you'll transport your articles; available parking; and suitable overnight lodging.

Assuming you have made good use of all the described marketing avenues, you have probably disposed of your treasures at a good price and ideally to people who will love, appreciate, and enjoy them as you have. So turn now to the good days ahead with a clear mind, a clean house, and the satisfaction of knowing that you did it YOUR WAY.

INDEX

NOTES

ADZE: A cutting tool with a thin, arched blade set at right angles to the handle; used chiefly for shaping wood.

ALLOY: The fusion of two or more metals, or of metals with nonmetals.

ANNUAL: An issue produced on a regular yearly schedule.

ART DECO: A decorative style of the 1920s and 1930s featuring bold outlines, streamlined form, and innovative materials such as plastic.

ARTICULATOR: A device united by means of a joint.

ART NOUVEAU: A decorative style of the late nineteenth century having sinuous lines and often foliation.

ARTISTS' PROOF: The first artpieces produced in a new edition, traditionally set aside for correction and personal use by the artist.

BACK ISSUE: Previously introduced art that is included in a series but not being currently produced.

BACKSTAMP: Information on the back of a limited edition collector article, including manufacturer, plate title, series name, artist, etc.

BAKELITE: A brand name for certain phenolic resins and products manufactured with these materials.

BAS RELIEF: Slightly raised designs that give depth and dimension to artpieces.

BISQUE (BISCUIT WARE): An unglazed porcelain or pottery with a matte texture resembling that of a biscuit.

BLUE BOOK: A book of specialized information such as market values of used cars.

BOOK PLATE: A book owner's identification label that is usually pasted to the inside front cover of a book.

BROADSIDE (BROADSHEET): A large sheet of paper printed originally on only one side for posting information, advertising, etc.

BUYER'S PREMIUM: A fee paid by the buyer (usually 10 percent) added to the final amount bid at an auction.

CANE: A fused glass rod used in paperweights and other artpieces.

CAPITAL GAIN PROPERTY: Includes property that does not provide a regular income.

CARNIVAL GLASS: A humble imitation of Tiffany and Carder hand-made artglass. It offers 1500+ patterns, many vivid colors, and objects and shapes for every purpose.

CARTOUCHE: An oval or oblong figure in which a sovereign's name is inscribed.

CASTING: Creating a mold from an original artpiece, then filling it with liquid clay to make a reproduction.

CERAMIC: Technically, any artpiece made by shaping and firing clay, e.g., porcelain, earthenware, terra-cotta, brick, etc.

CHINA: Better quality, finer ceramic ware; may or may not contain animal bone.

CLOISONNE: The product of a technique of firing and applying enamel cells onto thin metal strips. Or, an enamel decoration applied and fired in raised cells (e.g., soldered wire strips) on a usually metal background.

CONTINGENT FEES: When appraising, evaluating an article falsely high or low in order to obtain a benefit.

DAGUERREOTYPE: (After inventor Louis-Jacques-Mandé Daguerre.) An early photograph produced on a silver or silver-copper plate. This technique is now obsolete.

DATABASE: A collection of data organized for rapid research and retrieval.

DECAL (DECALCOMANIA): Also known as a transfer. A picture, design, or label on specially prepared paper to be transferred to glass, metal, wood, porcelain, etc.

DELTIOLOGIST: A student and collector of postcards.

DEPRESSION GLASS: Glass objects produced during the Depression using pressing molds. The products feature soft colors and opalescent sheens; their patterns are identified as Poppy, Dogwood, etc., according to the subject being represented.

DRAYDEL: A four-sided toy marked with Hebrew letters and spun like a top.

EARTHENWARE: Ceramic ware made of porous clay fired at low temperature.

EDITION: The total number of articles produced at one time.

EPHEMERA: Posters, valentines, tickets, menus, and other paper items that were originally intended to have only temporary or ad hoc interest.

EXONUMIA: Tokens and coins other than government issue, for example, medals, scrip, ingots, even wooden nickels.

FACET: A surface as of a cut gem.

FAIR MARKET VALUE: The price that is paid after negotiations between individual buyer and seller, as at a flea market, garage sale, etc.

FAUX: False. Often said of imitation pearls, or other gems.

FIGURAL: An artpiece fashioned in the shape of a human or animal.

FOLK ART: An art style of ethnic, peasant, or backwoods societies, also called "primitive art."

FORE-EDGE PAINTING: Picture on the front edge of a book page.

FOUNDRY MARK: The number, name, or letters identifying the foundry where a bronze or metal casting was produced.

FRETWORK: An ornamental pierced network or pattern, or work in relief.

GIGO: An acronym for "Garbage In Garbage Out" used on the computer.

GLAZE: The glossy, vitreous surface that is produced by covering the ceramic item with a coating that bonds to the piece during firing.

GRAPHIC: The art or technique of depicting something by painting, drawing, printmaking, or other method.

HALLMARK: A manufacturer's logo or identifying mark.

"HALO" EFFECT: An artifice that inflates an article's value by exhibiting it in a museum, featuring it in books and brochures, or publicizing it in newspapers, art magazines, and periodicals.

HAMMER PRICE: The term used to describe the successful bid.

HANDBLOWN GLASS: An artpiece fashioned by blowing rather than formed with a mold.

HOROLOGY: Clocks, watches, barometers, musical automata, etc.

HUMMER: A type of toy top.

INCISED: Writing or graphic design etched or carved into the surface of an artpiece to add detail and texture.

INRO: A small decorated Japanese container hung from an *obi* (sash) to hold medicines and small objects.

IRIDESCENCE: A play of lustrous, changing colors.

IRONSTONE CHINA: A hard, heavy, durable pottery developed in England in the early nineteenth century.

KNOCKED DOWN: The fall of the auctioneer's hammer after the final accepted bid: e.g., "Lot #6 was knocked down at $1,500."

LEAD CRYSTAL: The best glass, which must have a lead content of at least 24 percent.

LEXICON: The vocabulary of a particular subject.

LIMITED EDITION: Art produced in an arbitrarily limited quantity.

LIQUIDATOR: A person or firm that converts assets into cash.

LIST BROKER: A person or firm that develops and sells a list of sales prospects for a client.

LITHOGRAPH: A print or graphic produced by fixing the image on a stone or metal plate.

LOT: An item or group of items offered for sale as a unit.

LUCITE: A tradename for a transparent or translucent plastic.

MAJOLICA: Pottery glazed with an opaque tin enamel, usually highly decorated.

MANGLE: A machine for ironing laundry by passing it between heated rollers.

MASTER IMAGE: An original document, drawing, etc., from which copies are made.

MATRIX: The original mold, die, or form for shaping or producing art pieces.

MECCA: A place that attracts people with interests in common.

MECHANICALS: Valentines, cards, or other ephemera made with movable parts.

MEDIUM: The material or technical means of artistic expression.

MICROFILM: A film bearing a miniature photographic copy of printed or graphic matter; microfiche is a flat sheet of microfilms

MILLEFIORI: ("thousand flowers") Ornamental, especially paperweight, design produced by cutting innumerable cross sections of fused glass, vari-colored rod bundles.

MINT: Original, unused condition; MOB - Mint in original box.

MOLD: A hollow form or matrix for shaping something in molten or plastic state.

"MOONLIGHT": To work at an additional job after regular hours.

NETSUKE: A small Japanese carved figure, usually of ivory, decorating a man's sash.

NUMISMATIC: Pertaining to coins or paper money.

OENOPHILE: A lover or connoisseur of wines.

PIGGIN: A small wooden pail or tub with a handle formed by a continuation of one of the staves.

PORCELAIN: Strong, vitreous, translucent ceramic ware fired at high temperature.

PRIMARY MARKET: The first distribution network when the item is introduced at the "issue" price.

PROOF COIN SET: The first limited issue of coins struck from polished dies.

PROVENANCE: Documentation of a line of ownership.

RECAST: An item formed, modeled, or cast after the original issue.

REPLACEMENT COST: The amount that would have to be paid in a retail store or other commercial outlet for an item comparable in quality to the one insured.

RETIRED LIMITED EDITION: No longer being produced or available from the manufacturer.

REVERSE PAINTING ON GLASS: A design painted or transferred, usually by a multi-step process, onto the back of a glass base. Eglomisé is the French term for a special type of reverse painting on glass that is backed with gold or silver leaf foil.

RIVET: A metal pin or fastening device.

ROLLING STOCK: The wheeled vehicles of a railroad, including locomotives, freight cars, and passenger cars.

SAD IRON: A flat iron that is pointed at both ends and has a detachable handle.

"SCRAP": Unfilled leftover ad space offered by some magazines at discounted rates.

SECONDARY MARKET: A limited edition item that has completed its run and sold out at the issue price is now obtainable from the next, or second market, and subject to normal supply/demand factors.

SETTLE: A long seat or bench, usually wooden, with arms and a high back.

SULPHIDE: A paperweight, marble, or other art piece that has a figure embedded within the glass.

TEETOTUM: A small toy top usually inscribed with letters and used in the game "put and take."

TINTYPE: A picture made by a photographic process that used a black enameled metal plate. It quickly replaced the daguerreotype process because it was cheaper and simpler.

TOLEWARE: Finely painted and decorated tin pieces, sometimes called "Japanned ware."

TOUCHMARK: An identifying maker's mark impressed upon metal, usually pewter.

TRAMP ART: Furniture and accessories fashioned out of cigar boxes, fruit crates, etc., by itinerant craftsmen.

TRIVET: A metal stand, usually three-footed, for use under a hot dish or pot.

UNDERGLAZE: Painted or decorated artwork applied to a clay piece before its final glazing and firing.

VETTER: An expert appraiser or authenticator.

WHIRLIGIG: A child's toy in the shape of a figure having a whirling motion.

WICKER: Furniture material woven out of natural fibers, rattan bark, reeds, etc.

"WORM": The thread of a screw.

FURTHER READING

Certain of the following books may be out of print. A few of the references listed under "Marks" were published some time ago, and are no longer on bookstore shelves. This is understandable considering that their information represents scholarly, long-term research for articles that are very old, rare, and unusual.

If you are unable to find specific books, ask a book search company, known to book dealers, to help you or get in touch with:

Strand Bookstores
828 Broadway
New York, NY 10003
212-473-1452

To look up new and old books that are currently in print, refer to *Subject Guide to Books in Print*, published by R. R. Bowker Co.

GENERAL REFERENCE:

Auction Action, by Ralph Roberts,
TAB Books, Inc.

The Complete Guide to Buying and Selling at Auction,
by C. Hugh Hildesley, W. W. Norton.

Caring for Your Antiques and Collectibles, by Miriam Plans,
Antique Trader Books.

Cash for Your Undiscovered Treasures, by Dr. H. A. Hyman,
Treasure Hunt Publications.

Emyl Jenkins' Appraisal Book,
Crown Publishers, Inc.

Garage Sale Manual and Price Guide, by Morykan and Rinker,
Antique Trader Books.

Have Sale - Will Travel, Secrets of An Estate-Sale Agent,
by DeKlyne, Rising Eagle Publications.

I'll Buy That, by Dr. H. A. Hyman,
Treasure Hunt Publications.

Kovels' Guide to Buying, Selling,
and Fixing your Antiques and Collectibles,
Crown Publishers, Inc.

Maloney's Antiques and Collectibles Resource Directory,
Antique Trader Books.

The Official Directory to U.S. Flea Markets,
House of Collectibles (A Division of Ballantine Books).

Selling Your Valuables, by Jeanne Siegel,
Bonus Books.

Trash or Treasure, by Dr. H. A. Hyman,
Treasure Hunt Publications.

Wanted to Buy, Collector Books,
Schroeder Publishing Co.

Where to Sell Anything and Everything by Mail,
by Dr. H. A. Hyman, Treasure Hunt Publications.

MARKS

Bottle Makers and Their Marks, by Julian H. Toulose, Nelson.

The Complete Cut & Engraved Glass of Corning N.Y.,
by Sinclair and Spillman, Crown Publishers, Inc.

A Dictionary of Marks,
edited by Margaret MacDonald Taylor,
Hawthorne Books, Inc.

Doll Maker Marks, by Dawn Herlocher,
Antique Trader Books.

English China and its Marks, by Thomas H. Ormsbee,
Channel Press, Deerfield Editions, Ltd.

French Porcelain, by W. F. Honey,
Faber & Faber.

Glass: Art Nouveau to Art Deco, by Victor
Arvas, Rizzoli.

Handbook of Pottery and Porcelain Marks, by J. P. Cushion,
Faber & Faber.

Jade, Stone of Heaven, by Richard, Gump,
Doubleday & Co., Inc.

Kovels' American Silver Marks,
Crown Publishers, Inc.

Old Pewter: Its Makers and Marks, by Howard H. Cotterell,
Charles E. Tuttle.

SELECTED CATEGORIES

Art Nouveau Bing, by Gabriel P. Weisberg,
Harry N. Abrams, Inc.

Baseball Memorabilia Price Guide, Tuff Stuff Books.

The Bean Family Album, by Shawn Brecka,
Antique Trader Books.

Button, Button, by Peggy Ann Osborne,
Schiffer Publishing.

Collectible Costume Jewelry, by Simonds,
Collector Books.

Cookie Jar Book, by Schneider,
Schiffer Publishing.

Country Americana Price Guide, edited by Kyle Husfloen,
Antique Trader Books.

Five Hundred Years of Golf Balls,
by John F. Hotchkiss with a foreword by Arnold Palmer,
Antique Trader Books.

Folk Art Fish Decoys, by Donald J. Peterson,
Schiffer Publishing.

Furniture of the Depression Era (1920s-1940s), by Swedberg,
Collector Books.

Marbles, Big Book of, by Everett Grist,
Collector Books.

Official Price Guide to Hummel Figurines and Plates,
House of Collectibles (A Division of Ballentine Books).

Petretti's Coca-Cola Collectibles Price Guide, by Allan Petretti,
Antique Trader Books.

Pottery and Porcelain Ceramics Price Guide,
edited by Kyle Husfloen & Susan Cox,
Antique Trader Books.

Rockin' Records, by Jerry Osborne,
Antique Trader Books.

Toasters and Small Appliances, LW Books.

Toys and Prices, by Korbeck,
Antique Trader Books.

Two Hundred Patterns of Haviland China,
edited and published by Arlene Schleiger.

White Ironstone, by Jean Wetherhee,
Antique Trader Books.

Zippo, The Great American Lighter, by Poore,
Schiffer Publishing.

ABOUT THE AUTHOR

Miriam L. Plans was born in Brooklyn, New York. A graduate of George Washington University in Washington, D.C., she also studied at George Washington's Law School. Following a long career as a writer/editor/information specialist with the U.S. Depart-ment of Commerce (*Foreign Com-merce Weekly*) and other national agencies and departments, Plans relocated to Vero Beach, Florida, where she currently resides, and where her weekly column, "Collectors Corner," appears in local newspapers.

Plans' previous publishing activities include two books, *Caring for Your Antiques & Collectibles* and *Collectomania — Your Trinkets and Treasures,* as well as articles that have appeared in a variety of publications, including *Parents Magazine, Family Circle, Just Write,* and the Vero Beach, Florida, *Press Journal.*